What's Your FOOD SIGN?

What's Your FOOD SIGN?

How to Use Food Clues to Find Lasting Love

ALAN R. HIRSCH, M.D.
NEUROLOGIC DIRECTOR, SMELL & TASTE TREATMENT AND
RESEARCH FOUNDATION

STC Healthy Living
Stewart, Tabori & Chang

NEW YORK

Dedication
For manducating Noah, pantophagous Jack, glycolimiac Camryn, osophagous Marissa, and kalokagathical Debra. Wishing you everlasting eudemonia

• • •

Text copyright © 2006 Alan R. Hirsch, M.D.
Illustrations copyright © 2006 Michael Klein

Published in 2006 by Stewart, Tabori & Chang
An imprint of Harry N. Abrams, Inc.

Library of Congress Cataloging-in-Publication Data

Hirsch, Alan R.
What's your food sign? : how to use food clues to find lasting love / by Alan Hirsch.
p. cm.
ISBN 1-58479-425-9
1. Man-woman relationships. 2. Food habits. 3. Food preferences. 4. Dating (Social customs) I. Title.
HQ801.H53 2006
305.3—dc22
2005030722

Designed by Carole Goodman / Blue Anchor Design
Editor: Debora Yost

Notice
Celebrities mentioned in this book were not part of any study conducted by the Smell & Taste Treatment and Research Foundation; rather their public personas were used as illustrative examples. The author does not know their food/flavor preferences or their actual personality characteristics.

The text of this book was composed in ITC Avant Garde and ITC Lubalin Graph.

Printed in the United States of America
10 9 8 7 6 5 4 3 2 1

HNA ▌▌▌▌▌
harry n. abrams, inc.
a subsidiary of La Martinière Groupe

115 West 18th Street
New York, NY 10011
www.hnabooks.com

Contents

• • • • • • • • • • • • • •

WHAT'S YOUR FOOD SIGN?

Introduction:
Finding Mr. or
Miss Right

In her 1932 Pulitzer Prize–winning novel, *The Good Earth*, Pearl S. Buck wrote about a very old, traditional way to establish a marriage. Buck described a dowry system in which a father pre-arranges his daughter's marriage, with the future husband's family receiving money or valuable items in exchange. In 21st-century America, this is tantamount to selling your daughter into marriage.

Today, among some religions and in many parts of the world, arranged marriages still take place, but usually without the direct exchange of goods or money. The tradition still lingers among Hassidic Jews, in certain parts of India, Pakistan, Iran, and other Islamic countries, and

7

some isolated societies, but for the most part, it has disappeared from Western culture. Here, and in other parts of the developed world, young people assert their independence early and pay little or no attention to their parents' ideas or ideals about an appropriate mate. To them, the idea of an arranged marriage would be viewed as something alien, even scary.

> There are lessons to be learned from the fact that arranged marriages seldom fail.

Those who still practice the custom, however, could argue that much can be said in favor of arranged marriages. Whether we like the idea or not, history shows us that leaving the choice of a marriage partner to Mom and Dad led to stable marriages. Even today, statistics show that arranged marriages seldom fail—at least if we gauge failure by the divorce rate. Of course, there are many marriages that stay intact in which one or both partners are unhappy, but we have no way to measure failure based on "the scale of misery." In our modern culture, that does not count (at least officially). We call a marriage a success as long as a couple stays married, even when they live unhappily ever after. (Considering this, some might say divorce rates are deceptively low.)

Arranged marriages worked for many reasons, often having to do with a sense of community rather than with compatibility. In most cases, economic pressures and religious or cultural imperatives forced these marriages to stay intact, even if they were not particularly harmonious relationships.

Of course, we should not forget that in many cultures, women were viewed as "less than" men, which provided justification for their low status. Women were viewed as commodities and were assigned specific monetary values. No one thought it odd to bargain over the "price" for a wife. Having a female baby required a father to accumulate a dowry to pay off a future husband to take the daughter off his hands, thus transferring responsibility for this "item." Jane Austen's classic novel *Pride and Prejudice*, published in 1813, revolves around the dilemma of marrying off five daughters, with Austen slyly commenting on the pressure the young women felt to stop being a burden to their parents.

The perceived greater value of boys over girls continues to this day in some cultures. In China, for example, many more baby girls than baby boys are put up for adoption, and tragically, a higher incidence of female infanticide exists as well.

THE NEW WEDDING MARCH

It involved a long struggle, but American women have, for the most part, won the right to equal status with men.

(Clearly, women's journey isn't complete, and an "undertone" of lower status persists. For example, Harvard President Lawrence H. Summer found himself in hot water after suggesting that women may have less inherent aptitude for math and science than men do.) Surely, we can all agree that in our more egalitarian society, women are no longer viewed as chattel, and relationships and marriages cannot be built on a monetary exchange—at least overtly. We'd only be kidding ourselves if we believed that economic status is not a factor when choosing a mate—only now the choice belongs to both individuals.

> Middle-aged people make the same relationship mistakes as teenagers still learning the ropes of dating.

We have moved away from a system of arranged marriage to one in which we have found ourselves bobbing about in a sea of uncertainty and foundering relationships. In the United States, more than half of all marriages end in divorce. In many other countries, especially in the West, but even in some of the newly industrialized countries, divorce rates are approaching that of the United States. Obviously, we haven't fully adjusted to the relatively new system of selecting a mate based on the idealistic concept of romantic love. (though if you consider Greek drama and much of Shakespeare, it usually ends in disaster!).

Let's be optimistic and allow for the romantic notion of marrying for love. Nevertheless, other rational considerations come into play, such as "She is smart and successful" or "He's a family-man type" or "We are just so totally compatible!" Yes, it's a marriage made in Heaven! Or is it?

In reality, the answer to this is "not always," and on top of that, we don't always learn from past mistakes. Maturity doesn't appear to teach us much. Middle-aged adults seem to get together and break up (whether they marry or not) just as often as teenagers still learning the ropes of dating. Looking at it objectively, you'd have to say that romantic love is like a big mystery.

In a book about forming relationships, or better understanding existing ones, it may seem odd that I am talking about those that fail. But failure is what we want to avoid. A failed marriage or relationship is an emotionally painful experience that can leave permanent scars. Many people become reluctant to commit again to another person. Fear of failure can be paralyzing. It's much better and emotionally healthier to understand what makes relationships fail so you can avoid the same pitfalls when you're looking for a mate. Also, a deeper understanding may help the one you're in last!

WHO IS THIS STRANGER I MARRIED?

One often-cited reason for a failed relationship is that the couple discovers that they don't meet each other's expectations. "You just aren't who I thought you were," one says. "Yeah, well, neither are you," is the quick reply. There is an explanation for this. Most men and women have unrealistic expectations about the other person and the assumptions they make about the potential partner often turn out to be wrong.

> The movie *Sideways*
> is so funny because it
> is so realistic!

To get an exaggerated look at this kind of mistake, consider the 2005 Oscar-winning movie *Sideways.* This movie is a *realistic,* romantic black comedy because it deals with false expectations based on false perceptions, which come about because the men in the relationships use false pretenses to make women fall in love with them! It sounds like a wild ride, and it is, but the same scenarios occur in virtually all relationships—that's why the movie ends up being so funny.

When we meet a potential partner, we put our proverbial best foot forward, which, to be honest, is a "false pretense." Women may use more makeup than usual; men may dress better than they ordinarily do. We all try to appear as handsome or beautiful as can be, not to mention witty and pleasant. However, once the relationship is established, these façades break down and the true individual comes out.

When people live together, married or not, you know the honeymoon is over when men hang their suits in the back of the closet and start walking around in their underwear, and women forget about the makeup and drag out the sweat pants. In any relationship, people can sustain a false image for only so long. Unfortunately, when true personalities start to show, the partners can end up surprised and disappointed that the person beneath the façade—what I call a person's underlying essence—doesn't match their expectations. The partners begin to withdraw and, thus, the relationship dissolves. They may long for the "old days" and try to recapture the feeling of new love—those heady days when she laughed at all his jokes and he showed up with flowers. Sometimes, though, they look outside the relationship for satisfaction.

| Using false pretenses is something we all do in the mating game.

WHAT'S YOUR PERSONALITY TYPE?

If you don't want to end up disillusioned about a relationship, you need to accurately ferret out the true underlying essence or personality of the person you're courting *before* the relationship gets too deep, or even takes you down the path to marriage. To say that this is a big challenge is an understatement, because it is not something the typical person is trained to do, and especially not in school. As children, we learn very little about how to "read" people and understand individual personalities. Kids learn how to calculate the volume of a cube and how to dissect a frog, but it's the rare school that teaches important things like how to figure out who people really are. Yet these skills are essential to getting involved in the right relationships as we mature, and they play a big part in how happy we will be throughout life. Imagine how different marriages would be if all adults had acquired these skills when they were kids!

As they say, it's never too late to learn. Psychiatry has delineated general personality types, and has developed myriad ways to identify and label them. Personality type includes the characteristics responsible for how people think and respond to other people and situations. There are several personality types, but since each of us is unique, they do not fit all people like a glove.

There are terms we use that apply to an extreme personality type that may be "hidden." For example, you may be attracted to someone who appears to have a strong ego until you later discover that the person is really narcissistic, meaning the person has an ego so strong that he or she desires to be idolized. Another example is someone who enjoys solitude, which is a healthy trait. The extreme of this, in which the person must be isolated from others to feel whole or comlpete, may be considered schizoid. A life-of-the-party type may turn into a person who has to be the center of attention, a personality type we call histrionic.

MATCHMAKER, MATCHMAKER, FIND ME MY LOVE

Most people do not have extreme personalities; rather, they have a collection of different characteristics from a variety of personalities. As a layperson, figuring out these characteristics will be your biggest challenge. But it can be done. In psychiatry, we use a variety of personality tests as well as formal interviews to help determine someone's true personality, and this process often requires several sessions with the patient.

We don't as yet have a perfect system for matching compatible personalities, but it isn't for lack of trying. Just look at the explosion of computerized dating services, some of which try to determine personality types through questionnaires. All they are really doing is finding your "perfect match" through a process of elimination. The types of questionnaires psychiatrists use, on the other hand, are very involved and cannot be used in everyday settings.

FOOD TO THE RESCUE

At the Smell & Taste Treatment and Research Foundation in Chicago, we've found that after people lose their sense of smell (often as a result of a head injury), a personality change occurs, and beyond that, their preferences for food change, too. As odd as that probably sounds, given what we know about the brain, these phenomena make sense.

The frontal lobe is the part of the brain that is involved with personality, and the limbic system, the "emotional brain," is located in the same area of the brain where the sense of smell is localized (the olfactory lobe). Since head trauma can damage both areas of the brain, it is plausible that a corresponding alteration of both personality and food preferences can result, and that food preferences and personality are interconnected in some way.

WHAT'S YOUR FOOD SIGN?

I didn't give this a great deal of thought until we conducted a study to find out if using odors in a particular way could help facilitate weight loss. The study included 3,193 people and lasted for 6 months. During that time, we had these individuals inhale different odors such as banana, green apple, and peppermint. We found that inhaling these odors suppressed their appetites and induced impressive weight loss—an average of 30 pounds over the course of 6 months.

We found that many women—86 percent of the people in the study were women—described cravings, especially for chocolate, at varying times during their menstrual cycle. This is understandable because chocolate contains a variety of chemicals such as phenylethylamine, tyramine, caffeine, xanthine, and others, some of which act as precursors to serotonin, a neurotransmitter in the brain. A deficiency of serotonin is associated with depression, thus chocolate may act as a natural antidepressant, almost like a mini-Prozac. Therefore, it's possible that women's craving for chocolate is the body's attempt to self-medicate underlying depression associated with a phase of the menstrual cycle.

A logical question followed: If women crave chocolate when they are mildly depressed, does it mean that other kinds of cravings are indicative of their personalities and mood states? Could stable preferences for food provide clues to true underlying personality? That was the beginning of my investigation of food preferences in relation to personality type.

FOOD AND PERSONALITY SCIENCE

We began our food and personality research by using already-existing personality tests such as the MMPI-II (Minnesota Multiphasic Personality Inventory), the MCMI (Millon Clinical Multiaxial Inventory), the BDI (Beck Depression Inventory), the Zung Depression Scale, and the Zung Anxiety Scale. These tests involve over 1,000 questions relating to different aspects of a person's life. From the answers to the questions, we were able to determine specific character and personality traits.

With this information in hand, we then went back and looked at the food preferences of the individuals who answered the questionnaires, using what is known as a forced-choice method. For example, our test subjects were asked to choose a specific ice cream flavor among five or six choices. We did the same for spices and certain groups of fruits and vegetables. In other words, individuals had to choose which food they liked the most from only those foods items on the list.

The most interesting part came next. We took the results of the initial personality tests and performed an analysis to see if a correlation existed between a preference for a particular food and a specific personality trait. We found out that for some foods this was impossible to do. For example, so many people said they liked chocolate that we had to drop that specific choice from the list (we solved this problem in subsequent studies by subdividing the chocolate into light versus dark and hollow versus solid, as in chocolate Easter candy).

After correlating food preference and personality, we took another step and looked at the spouses of those who had participated in the study. The purpose was to find out how their food preferences related to those of their mates. We were able to statistically correlate food preferences of the spouses as well. We intentionally included in the study people who had been married for at least a year—a statistical indicator of a stable romantic relationship. We found a correlation between certain food preferences and these stable relationships.

One of the drawbacks of this methodology was that it was a retrospective study, meaning that the participants were already married for at least a year prior to being queried about their food preferences. Since men and women tend to be influenced by their partners' food choices, they may try foods the other person introduces. So over time, those in stable relationships adopt similar food preferences. This introduced possible, but unavoidable, bias to the study. Despite this limitation, I have observed a link between food and personality, one that may be a key to compatibility. In the following pages, I will share this information with you and show you how to read personality and use food preferences to find everlasting love. Be forewarned: It involves finding out who you really are, too!

After you read this book, I expect that old opening line "What's your sign?" will be replaced with "What's your food sign?" But this time, the answer will actually mean something! I wrote this book to be a new and fun way to make a quick assessment of other people and to determine with whom you may be most compatible. Use it to find your own true self and to help you in your search for someone special. Share it with your friends. Have fun with it at parties. Use it to predict the compatibility of new relationships. You'll be amazed at how much you can learn just by watching what your date orders for lunch!

ALAN R. HIRSCH, M.D.

Neurologic Director
Smell & Taste Treatment and Research Foundation
Chicago

January 2006

1

LOVE AT FIRST BITE:
THE DILEMMA OF
COMPATIBILITY

We are genetically programmed **to be** superficial when it comes to physical attraction. We also tend to be superficial when on a date. It all makes for a very challenging way to find true love.

• • • • •

When we go about choosing someone to date or marry, what are the characteristics we look for? Most people love this question because it gives them a chance to sound "deep" and "knowing." People cringe at the thought of sounding superficial. So, I hope it doesn't upset you to learn that, in reality, we are a very superficial species. One study after another confirmed the truth behind the motto, "Beauty can't be beat." Overwhelmingly, people attempt to date or marry those who reach society's ideal of beauty.

In our society, beauty is defined as an attractive face—perfect symmetry—and a slender body. The taller, the better, too. Things like breast size in women and muscularity in men are two other often-sought-after traits.

> One study indicates
> that men really do
> prefer blondes.

Evidence of our superficial preferences goes beyond romance and sex. In modern presidential elections in which neither candidate is an incumbent, the man who is taller or appears taller almost always wins, because tallness is considered a desirable trait and is a sign of power and superiority. The candidates for many other elected positions who meet this perception of masculine beauty ("machoesque") also generally win. These candidates appear to be more likely to succeed regardless of their positions on the issues. We can generalize and say that in public life, tall men have an advantage over shorter competitors. It's yet to be seen how height will influence the outcome of presidential races when one or both candidates is a woman!

This preference for youthful-looking, tall presidents has been discussed in political literature for decades, and was analyzed in the 1968 book *The Selling of the President*, by Joe McGinnis. McGinnis's book focused on the way in which Richard Nixon was "marketed" in order to win the election. It was a ploy that ushered in the kind of sophisticated use of media we see in presidential campaigns today. The book also revealed the uncomfortable truth that we believe we vote for "positions" and perceived character traits, such as trustworthiness, but in reality, we cast our votes based on a more visceral concept of attractiveness.

This visual appeal crosses the boundaries into our personal relationships—bosses, friends, coworkers, and so forth, and it especially applies to the search for romance.

Hey,
Good Lookin'

Though we don't consciously realize it, our everyday interactions are influenced by standards of attractiveness. For example, a man will step in and help change a flat tire for a woman with blonde hair more often than he will for the same woman who dyes her hair black. A woman will choose to date a taller man over a short man who is both more educated and socially desirable. For example, in one study, women consistently chose to date a tall unemployed laborer or even a drug dealer over a successful neurosurgeon of short stature.

It's an uncomfortable notion, but attractiveness also has a big influence on who gets accepted into better schools and who gets hired for the best jobs. In hiring, to use one example, studies have shown that the same individual who appears more beautiful or handsome—the ideal of feminine and masculine attractiveness—will be hired over the same person who has been disguised to appear less physically attractive, but presents better credentials.

It gets worse! In instances where two individuals perform identical work, the attractive person will be perceived as doing a superior job. This principle applies not just to the business environment, but also in the grading practices among college professors and teachers in an academic environment.

> Forget the car!
> Women will always
> go for the taller guy.

This principle has even invaded the world of medicine. A variety of studies suggest that when patients think a physician is handsome or beautiful, in terms of both dress and facial appearance, they believe that the doctor is more competent and more likely to provide correct information.

Patients of both sexes are more likely to confide their medical information and reveal personal information to these good-looking doctors.

Good looks play a leading role in our search for a mate.

The studies imply the awkward truth that we have a preconceived notion that beauty is skin deep—that external beauty signifies internal goodness or beauty.

This makes some evolutionary sense since several major genetic defects are manifested through changes in body, and through abnormalities in skin, shape, asymmetries, and hemiatrophy (meaning that one side of the body is smaller than the other side). These individuals can be perceived as having genetic "defects" that could prevent successful procreation. In other words, this means they are less desirable as potential mates. So, it's likely that our pursuit of beauty may be based on evolution. If you look at it this way, we are not shallow after all!

In fact, the perception that symmetry is beautiful crosses cultures and has been documented throughout history. When something like this is universal and endures over time, it suggests that a strong evolutionary bias exists toward it. So, we can't write it off by claiming that slick magazines are shoving the ideals of beauty in our faces. They push beauty because it is what we want to look at!

Sniffing
for Love

Basically, if you smell good, people perceive you as good; if you smell bad, people perceive you as bad. The way a person smells is the way we interpret someone's underlying essence. In religious history, saints were said to have had ethereal and heavenly smells even in death; those viewed as evil were said to smell like sulfur.

> Your odor sends a
> signal of your true
> underlying essence.

This tendency to judge based on the way something or someone smells has led to the proliferation of a vast industry of perfumes and other scented products. Upon introduction, your sense of smell directly influences whether or not you like a new person, and the way you smell influences him or her, too. If you smell good, you are more likely to be seen as good—morally upstanding.

Though we are not consciously aware of it, every person has a unique odor "signature." An individual's scent is like an odor fingerprint that is based on our specific DNA structure. A man who loves a woman "like a sister," or a woman who loves a man "like a brother," could mean that the person's odor signature is just not appealing enough to consider a stronger emotion. It is nature's way of preventing unions of DNA profiles that are too much alike. Put simply, one reason we don't mate with family members is that genetic defects are more likely to occur when DNA is too similar.

> Sexual chemistry is largely due to an unconscious attraction to the other person's odor.

You could say that by "sniffing" for a mate, we are promoting genetic diversity and human survival, while also reducing the risk of genetic mutations. Our odor signature is important in our interactions with others and plays an important role in whether or not we find someone appealing or sexually arousing. What we call sexual chemistry may in fact be largely due to our unconscious response to the other person's odor signature.

MEN AND **PUMPKIN PIE**

Speaking of romantic chemistry, our studies found that men and women are very different when it comes to sexually arousing smells. We found that the number-one odor that enhances sexual arousal in men is a combination of lavender and pumpkin pie. It increased penile blood flow by 40 percent compared to a combination of doughnuts and black licorice, which caused a 31.5 percent increase, and doughnuts and pumpkin pie, which enhanced penile blood flow 20 percent. So, the adage "the way to a man's heart is through his stomach" should probably be changed to "the way to a man's heart is through his nose."

The same study found that sexually arousing scents can change as a person ages. For example, the older the man, the greater the effect vanilla has on sexual arousal.

Those who claimed to have the most sexually satisfying relationships demonstrated the greatest penile response with the aroma of strawberry. Those who engaged frequently in sexual intercourse showed the greatest response to the scents of lavender, oriental spice, and cola. Perfumes, however, didn't do much at all, increasing penile blood flow by only a median of 3 percent—lower than the scent of cheese pizza (5 percent) and buttered popcorn (9 percent).

> As a man ages, he begins to find the scent of vanilla sexually arousing.

For women, the number-one odor that enhanced female sexual arousal was a combination of Good & Plenty candy and cucumber. Good & Plenty combined with banana nut bread also had positive effects.

In men, every single odor we tested enhanced penile

What Turns Men On?

· ·

Not perfume! At The Smell & Taste Treatment and Research Foundation we studied what odors cause sexual arousal in men, and perfume came in dead last—even after pizza.

Here is what we found turned men on, measured by the increase in penile blood flow:

> Lavender and pumpkin pie: 40%
>
> Doughnuts and black licorice: 31.5%
>
> Doughnuts and pumpkin pie: 20%
>
> Buttered popcorn: 9%
>
> Cheese pizza: 5%
>
> Perfume: 3%

blood flow to some extent, which suggests a very resilient organ. On the other hand, some odors inhibited female sexual arousal, including the smell of barbecued meat and cherries. Som men's colognes also can turn women off.

We don't know why these odors reduce sexual arousal in women. Maybe the smell of cherries induces a memory of being ill and medicated with cherry cough syrup as a child. Or, perhaps men's cologne reminds women of too many negative experiences with men.

The exact reasons why certain odors have an effect on sexual stimulation remains unknown, but our data imply that certain odors can play a major role in your love life. However, and this is key: *Both the external visual and odor "pictures" do not necessarily represent a person's true personality that is hiding within.*

Kissing:
Show and Tell

Romantic kissing is another area that involves smell and taste, but not necessarily in the obvious ways. When two people kiss, saliva moves from one person to the other, and saliva has a specific taste of protein that represents that person's unique DNA. There is a belief that the taste of another's DNA will be unpleasant if the individuals' genes are too similar. It's the reason why you instinctively turn up your nose at the idea of kissing your brother or sister.

Our foundation did a study designed to compare the preferred taste of kisses shared by 200 couples on dates and kisses shared by 200 married couples. Both married and single women preferred their husband's or date's kisses to taste like peppermint and spearmint. Similarly, the married men preferred their wife's kiss to taste like mint.

> Married men prefer
> minty kisses, whereas sin-
> gle men like kisses that
> taste like alcohol.

On the other hand, single men preferred their dates' kisses to taste of alcohol. This may represent a learned response, perhaps because the men had more successful dating experiences when the women drank alcohol.

Masked
Appeal

Getting to know a person's true underlying essence is not as easy as it used to be. We have long been a sanitized culture and the genetic clues that might tip us in the direction of Mr. Right or away from Miss Wrong have been masked by water, soap, perfume, toothpaste, breath strips, and mouthwash, just to name a few. So what we are instinctually interpreting as external stimuli, such as a person's natural breath odor, is really a masked odor sending out false signals. In the course of human history, this is a relatively new dilemma.

In the days before we became such an egalitarian society, people who worked in the fields would have a field smell, those who worked in the stockyards would have a stockyard smell, and those who worked in an industry would have a smell specific to that industry. But today, we can all smell alike. As it turns out, running water has become the great equalizer, quite possibly the most democratizing component of society, more so than even the United States Constitution, or the Magna Carta.

Yet, the body is still genetically programmed to sniff out a mate. We can look at this as a kind of setup. People can easily believe a relationship is made in heaven because: "He's so handsome" or "She smells so good." Then one day, they discover that the marriage is not working because they are not who their olfactory signature portrayed them to be. This causes false expectations and, thus, predisposes them to incompatibility, which is most commonly cited as the reason approximately half of all marriages end in divorce, often in the first year.

> The human body is genetically programmed to sniff out another person's real personality.

Why are so many people so wrong? To a great extent, it's because we base compatibility on an idealized view of love that does not meet reality. By the time a person realizes that the superficial characteristics of new-found love do not truly represent the person's underlying personality, they are well into the relationship. The phrase "the honeymoon is over" did not come out of nowhere. The honeymoon phase ends about the time a couple realizes that they didn't marry who they thought they did.

Speaking in evolutionary terms, this realization takes approximately 1 year, long enough for the cave woman to become pregnant and bear a child, at which point the role of the caveman becomes less important. In our modern life, and I suspect in arranged marriages, too, great disappointment sets in when the so-called "bloom is off the rose," which also takes about a year—and is the reason many marriages fall apart.

So, in reality, all marriages "end" after the first year, if you consider that people marry with an ill-conceived idea of their spouse's true nature and personality. For some, a new marriage within the marriage is possible and the couple moves on. However, people who get divorced often say that they just didn't marry the person they thought they were marrying. Truth is, the other person didn't change at all.

You Are
Who You Are

Personalities don't change. Except in extraordinary, rare circumstances, or life-threatening situations, personalities take hold by about age 7 and remain stable throughout life. What actually changes in a marriage is a mate's perception and expectations when he or she finally learns what the spouse's true underlying personality is like. It would save a lot of heartache to find this out before getting too serious or even married.

This book is about ways to learn critical information ahead of time. Of course, you could give your dates surveys and personality tests, but most people would balk at being asked hundreds of questions. Going through years of training to become a psychoanalyst would work, too, but that's hardly a practical solution. I and my colleagues at the Smell & Taste Research and Treatment Foundation devised techniques that involve the senses of smell or taste—and more specifically, food preferences: We have found scientific evidence that you can gain great insight into people's underlying personalities by observing the kinds of foods they prefer. So, set up a dinner date, meet for drinks, get tickets to a baseball game and order snacks, or just go out for an old-fashioned ice cream date. But first, learn to interpret what their food choices will be telling you, based on our scientific research.

The information you'll find in this book pays special attention to romantic compatibility and will add a useful and fun dimension in your search for a perfect partner—the person with whom you, if you do your homework, will ultimately share a successful long-term relationship.

2

SQUARE PEGS, ROUND HOLES: MEASURING WHO YOU REALLY ARE

Follow the old adage "you can't judge a book by its cover," because people, both consciously and unconsciously, will go to great length to hide their true selves.

• • • • •

When I was applying to medical school at the University of Michigan, I recall taking a test that, although I never knew its actual name, my classmates and I referred to as the raw carrot test. We gave it that nickname because one of the questions on the test was: Do you like raw carrots? *Yes or no.*

All the questions were presented in a forced-choice manner, meaning we had to pick among a group of answers. Multiple choice, true/false, and yes/no questions force a choice. Some of them appeared to be about as relevant to medical school as our like or dislike of carrots. We were even asked if we read auto mechanics magazines. *Yes or no.*

Obviously, these questions had nothing to do with anything we would be involved with in our academic program, yet based on responses to these questions, the test was able to statistically predict the likelihood of our success in medical school. This demonstrates that different personality traits can be measured and statistically correlated to future performance. This opened my eyes to the possibility that every single thing we do leaves a "fingerprint" of our personalities: the way we walk and talk, the direction we comb our hair, the color tie or the type of jewelry we choose to wear, the type of car we drive–even our preference for raw carrots. Even the manner in which we drink our coffee reveals something about us. Do we gulp, sip, or slurp? Maybe we let it sit in the cup and get cold.

Those professionally involved in predicting behavior often use ordinary activities to help define personality characteristics. Psychiatrists are interested in identifying a person's personality type because certain personalities are predictive of certain behaviors. This is important because personalities remain stable and don't change much over a lifetime.

For example, those who are more introspective will, when confronted with personality test questions, think about their responses before they answer. Those who are extroverted will respond more quickly and even aggressively. Optimists generally choose a path that suggests success, but pessimists will be more defensive in their responses. The point of tests such as the "raw carrot test" is to determine underlying personality traits in order to predict how people will react in future situations.

> Every gesture—even the manner in which you drink your coffee—reveals something about you.

Personality tests are often used to screen people for specific employment positions. For example, the U.S. Department of Defense might want to know what type of personality their soldiers have, especially if they could end up in a situation in which they were told to push the button to launch a nuclear missile. Or a hospital needs to know, when confronted with a life-threatening situation in the emergency room, if an emergency room doctor is the kind of person who would be able to perform a fast tracheotomy to save a patient's life.

Even with all the tests, future behavior is one of the most difficult things to predict. For example, the one trait psychiatrists have tried to predict is the possibility or likelihood that a certain person will attempt to commit an act of

violence in the future. In reality, though, the best predictor of future violence is a history of past violence. We can identify someone's past aggressive behaviors as characteristic of a sociopathic personality; however, personality traits in and of themselves are not as good a predictor of future violent behavior as are past violent acts. In other words, if we could predict future violent behavior, perhaps we could find mechanisms to prevent it.

If you recall the movie *Minority Report*, three psychic individuals, called precogs, were able to predict future violent behavior because they could read minds and see intention before the action was carried out. Then the police, through the character played by Tom Cruise, were able to arrest the perpetrators before the behavior occurred. However, that's a movie, and science has to deal with reality.

If you've ever taken a psychological test as part of a job application, even for a job in a retail store or a restaurant, then the test was probably designed to determine if you are prone to shoplift or steal. Behavioral science now even influences the way juries are selected, and great resources go into discovering underlying personality traits of the individuals on a jury, as shown in the movie *Runaway Jury*. Attempting to predict behavior using scientific research methods is nothing new; various techniques have been tried for well over 100 years.

Tests and
Limitations

Many tests are available to help determine a personality type, and among the best are the MMPI and MCMI that I mentioned in the introduction. Their biggest drawback is that they require several hours to complete. However, they have been validated over time and are quite accurate in pinpointing personality disorders and personality traits.

However, even as good as the tests are, and as good as psychiatry is in determining a personality type, people are not robots. Certain circumstances and situations can sometimes make a person do things or make decisions that are contrary to their underlying personality or are not consistent with their everyday behavior.

For example, in the movie *Hero*, Dustin Hoffman plays a criminal, but when a plane crashes, another aspect of his personality is revealed as he heroically saves hundreds of people on the airplane. In real life, we hear about prisoners who volunteer to help out during natural disasters such as floods or earthquakes. Virtually everyone wanted to help in some way during our period of national shock following September 11, 2001, including some street gang members, many of whom the average citizen may have feared on any other day.

Currently, personality tests are the best tools we have, with the following caveat: Individuals' actions do not always follow their personality type, so simply identifying a personality type does not necessarily mean that their actions are always going to reflect that specific personality profile.

The type of personality tests you will find in this book are based on the same kinds of tests used in psychiatry and research. While it's clear that a whole battery of tests would be more accurate, this would require herculean efforts in time and cost, including the need to have a psychiatrist or psychologist interpret the test.

> A big problem in the search for a spouse is that we often change our ideal of a perfect partner *after* we are married.

It is absurd to think that any potential partners (employers, babysitters, auto mechanics, financial advisors, and even friends) would undergo hours of personality testing just so we could evaluate the results and then find a perfect match. That sounds like a scene in a romantic comedy, doesn't it? But we can do the next best thing and use a quick-and-dirty method—like watch what your date eats for lunch.

At our foundation, we originally designed our food preference research as a tool for psychiatrists to use to help determine the personalities of their patients. However, this tool is so intriguing that when word of it spread, we received requests to develop similar tests for use in other areas, including employment agencies that now use it as part of their screening process.

Likewise, food preferences can be used by the average person to assess potential romantic partners. Of course, no one can say for sure which personality types are perfectly compatible. We all say we want completely virtuous, always empathetic, and unusually understanding individuals. In other words, we want perfection. The problem is, people fitting that description don't exist.

One of the glitches in our plan to find a perfect partner is that we often change our ideal of what we consider a perfect partner after we have married. For instance, women frequently gain a large amount of weight after they marry, because their husbands may subconsciously want them to become heavy, so they subtly promote their spouse's weight gain.

Why would this be the case? Because certain men prefer that their wives be less attractive to other men. In their minds, the extra weight serves as a deterrent and eases his worry that she will stray.

When Opposites Attract

Just how similar a couple should be in their personality traits is still up for debate. The logical answer seems to be, and probably always will be, it depends. For instance, an element of narcissism is in play. We like ourselves, and therefore we tend to like people in whom we see ourselves. This is why in certain settings, such as a job interview, if you are wearing the same cologne as the interviewer, that person unconsciously will tend to have a favorable reaction to you.

This preference for self proves true in some opposite sex situations. Let's use the job interview as an example. If you are a male and smell more like the female interviewer, she will like you more. On the other hand, studies show that if you are a woman being interviewed by a male, any perfume you wear will be viewed in the negative, possibly because the interviewer tends to see that as an attempt to manipulate him.

> Two people who are alike will be attracted to each other—but does it mean they are *meant* for each other?

We can extend this theory to dating. Two people who see themselves as similar tend to believe they are compatible— you could say they "take to each other." Of course they do! It's like looking at a version of themselves—and they like that. People truly are inherently narcissistic. Birds of a feather flock together.

There is a counter theory that opposite personalities are most compatible. According to this theory, an extrovert should pair up with an introvert, a narcissist should end up with a person with a more dependent personality, and an aggressive person should be with a passive one. The idea here is that these opposites will complement each other.

Just because two people are alike is not enough to predict long-term happiness. In some long-term marriages, the two personalities are worlds apart, yet the marriages have been stable for decades. Keep in mind, however, the caveat

WHAT'S YOUR FOOD SIGN?

that a long-term marriage isn't necessarily a happy one. Since each individual relationship is unique, we can only measure how compatible different personality types are by whether they remain in the relationship or not.

Personalities
in Disguise

Beauty is a trait that influences the way we respond to and evaluate others. This natural tendency has been muddled by modern life because there are so many ways in which we can alter our appearance.

Cosmetics represent one way, and clothing plays a role, too. Vertical stripes are supposed to induce an optical illusion that can make a person look thinner. Likewise, most of us will adopt a particular posture or sit in a certain way to minimize our asymmetry, or faults, and maximize our physical attributes.

Our studies found that when women wear an aroma that smells somewhat like mixed floral scent combined with Old Spice, men perceive them as thinner by an average of 12 pounds. This suggests that olfactory influences can even further help create illusions of visual beauty. We might call them the olfactory equivalents of vertical stripes.

> A woman wearing the scent of mixed flowers combined with Old Spice gives a man the perception that she is thinner than she really is. The scent of grapefruit makes her appear younger.

The concept of the ideal beauty, as portrayed by Madison Avenue, correlates beauty with youth. Why this is so is, again, based in evolution because youth implies fertility, and to preserve the species, we need to reproduce. Therefore, since youthfulness is more appealing, people do all sorts of things to portray themselves as being younger.

That's one reason Botox treatments and face-lifts are so popular. It's also why men and women alike choose clothes they hope will make them appear more youthful. One of our other studies found that the scent of pink grapefruit makes men perceive women as approximately 6 years younger.

I mention these things because sensory mechanisms are used to hide certain aspects of our appearance and enhance others. For millennia there have been attempts to change the visual image to meet the accepted ideal. These are likely to continue because no matter how much we spout platitudes like *"you can't judge a book by its cover,"* in reality, this is exactly what we should do!

3

LOVE AT FIRST SNIFF: THE NOSE AND THE SURVIVAL OF THE SPECIES

Though you are not physically aware of it, your sense of smell plays a big role in your choice of mate—and in ways that can be challenging.

• • • • •

We have a strong cultural assumption that love at first sight is not only a reality, but more common than most people think. If the truth be known, we really should be talking about love at first sniff.

My colleagues and I have found a link between the sense of smell and sexual arousal. Though love and attraction involve more than just sexual arousal, our studies show that we cannot discount the fact that smell plays a central role in attraction. A few theories may explain this.

One reason involves basic anatomy. The part of the brain that controls romantic feelings and love, including sexual desire, is located in the limbic system. Specifically, sexual desire has its root in the septal nucleus, more commonly known as the arousal center, of the limbic lobe of the brain, which is directly connected to the olfactory bulb at the top of the nose. When the septal nucleus in a male squirrel monkey is electrically stimulated, an erection occurs. The interconnections between the smell receptors and the arousal center explain the link between scents and sexual arousal. These same pathways exist in humans.

Smell is the only sense that has a direct link to the limbic lobe, the emotional center of the brain. The cortex, the area of the brain that directs intellectual activities, also processes the senses of sight, sound, and touch prior to linking to the limbic system. Smell is exactly the opposite. An odor first projects to the limbic lobe and then to the cortex. For example, if you detect an odor, you decide if you like or dislike it even before you know what it is. But if you see an object, such as a cow or a house, you identify it first, and then evaluate or judge it.

It may seem odd to you that I am talking a lot about the sense of smell in a book that is supposed to help you find true love by observing what people like to eat. But smell is essential because without it, you'd be missing out on an important tool—that is, the ability to sniff out someone special. In fact, you use your sense of smell all the time in your search for romance. It's just that you are not consciously aware of it. Science was not the first to notice this. Archeological evidence and ancient literature confirms that in the early civilizations of Pompeii, Egypt, and China, a variety of smells were associated with sexuality.

> The sense of smell plays a key role in romantic and sexual interest.

About 100 years ago Sigmund Freud offered up the notion that we must repress our olfactory instincts if we want to have a civilized society. In his view, only the so-called primitive societies "celebrated" the sense of smell and its obvious connection to sexuality. Freud postulated that it was essential to ignore the sense of smell, or else people would walk around sexually excited all the time. Clearly, Western culture, along with everyone else in the world, has ignored this piece of advice. One look at a cosmetic counter tells us that we are enjoying our sense of smell more than ever!

What Turns
Men On

In treating patients at the Smell & Taste Treatment and Research Foundation, we found that about a quarter of our patients who had lost their sense of smell had also developed some type of sexual dysfunction. We wanted to find out if the loss of the ability to smell contributed to eventual sexual difficulties. This is what led to our studies of penile and vaginal blood flow that I discussed briefly in chapter 1.

Our early studies were done on male medical students, and we used surgical masks to introduce them to a variety of scents. The masks were impregnated with the scents and, in a randomized fashion, the medical students inhaled them. In research such as this, scientists always use a control, meaning, in this case, an odor that theoretically would have no influence on sexual arousal and could be used as the baseline on which to measure responses to other odors. We used baked cinnamon buns as the control odor because we believed it would have no effect at all.

Lo and behold, the baked cinnamon buns had a greater effect on penile blood flow than all perfumes we tested combined. At first, we didn't know what to make of this. Could it simply mean that medical students are always hungry? Soon after, we studied males in the general population ranging in age from 18 to 64. As before, we used all kinds of floral scents and perfumes, but this time, we included more food items.

As you saw in Chapter 1, the number-one odor that

enhances penile blood flow is a combination of lavender and pumpkin pie; number two is a combination of dough-nuts and black licorice; and number three is a combination of pumpkin pie and doughnuts. Food scents were more sexually stimulating to men than expensive perfumes that are introduced with millions of dollars worth of advertising— a joke on all of us.

> Men found the smell of pumpkin pie more sexually arousing than any perfume.

We found some individual variations, but none that challenged the overall outcome. We found that:

* The older the man, the greater effect vanilla had on penile blood flow.

* Men who reported the greatest degree of satisfaction with their sex lives had the greatest response to the scent of strawberries.

* Men who were the most sexually active showed the greatest increase in penile blood flow with lavender, oriental spice, and cola.

Over and over, we found that any food we tested got some kind of physical reaction from men. Even smells, such as the aroma of buttered popcorn or cheese pizza, among the more common everyday smells in our culture, out-performed perfumes. But it is significant that the big winners—lavender and pumpkin pie—increased penile blood flow by 40 percent, while perfumes increased it by only 3 percent, a substantial difference!

The exact mechanism that causes the brain to respond to a particular odor remains unclear, although we've come up with several explanations. It's possible that the odors we used in our studies stimulated the septal nucleus, thus inducing arousal. However, it's also possible that the odors acted in a psychological way. Maybe the men's responses to the smells were essentially a Pavlovian (conditioned) response, meaning that a particular scent triggered the men to recall a state or mood they associated with past experiences of being sexually aroused.

It is also possible that the odors induced olfactory-evoked nostalgia. We've all had the experience of inhaling a scent that brings up a vivid, often emotionally charged, memory from childhood. Perhaps this happened to the men we tested who were exposed to lavender and pumpkin pie. However, when we analyzed that area too deeply, it got a little Oedipal—food smells from childhood associated with mothers and grandmothers? We didn't think that quite told the whole story.

> **The smell of food has the ability to arouse a man even when he is asleep.**

We also hypothesized that food scents induced sexual arousal because they reduced anxiety, and promoted a more natural, relaxed state, which then acted to disinterest the men, thus allowing sexual arousal. Or, maybe the odors work on the reticular activating system (RAS), which is the part of the brain that makes us more awake and alert. By being more awake and alert, the men became more aware of the sexual cues around them. But we discounted this theory after we discovered that the scents caused an arousal reaction in the men whether they were awake or asleep. Some of the men slept through the entire study, even when we changed the odors and measured their blood pressure (one cuff on the arm and a smaller cuff on the penis). So, wide awake or dead to the world, lavender and pumpkin pie worked their "magic."

It's unlikely that pumpkin pie receptors actually exist in the nose, but we can't ignore the suggestion that these odors have a strong impact beyond a conscious psychological effect.

What Turns
Women On

After we completed the study on what turns men on and published the results, many men asked how soon we'd be studying women. One bluntly queried, "Who cares what arouses men? What arouses women?"

At that time, female sexual arousal, as measured by vaginal blood flow in response to the effect of aromas, had never been objectively, physiologically assessed. You may find this hard to believe, considering that the fragrance industry spends five billion dollars a year selling perfumes on the basis of sex appeal!

The first obstacle was finding volunteers. We couldn't just go up to women on the street and ask if they would mind if we measured their vaginal blood flow in the name of science. (No surprise that we had no trouble finding male volunteers.) We ended up recruiting many of our female volunteers by talking about the study on The Loop, a Chicago radio station.

Vaginal blood flow was measured by using a pho-tophlethysmograph, a sterile tamponlike device that when inserted in the vagina, determines changes in blood flow. This correlates with the level of sexual arousal. We entered this study with two different hypotheses. The first was that the same kind of food odors that arouse men would arouse women, since it made no evolutionary sense that one sex would be aroused while the other wouldn't. But, we also had a counter-hypothesis. Since women in our society are involved in buying, cooking, serving, and cleaning up food, we wouldn't expect food to be sexually exciting to them. In fact, it was quite possible that food odors might actually inhibit sexual arousal in women. In short, we'd covered all the bases.

Food odors enhanced vaginal blood flow—but not the same food smells that excited the men. The odor that induced the greatest increase in vaginal blood flow was a combination of Good & Plenty candy and cucumber, although a combination of Good & Plenty and banana-nut bread had positive effects, too.

Some differences between men and women did become clear. *Every* odor we tested enhanced penile blood flow to some degree. Not so for women. In fact, we found a few odors actually inhibited sexual arousal in women, including the smell of cherries, barbecued roasted meat, and men's cologne.

> The smell of men's cologne inhibited sexual arousal in women.

We didn't know for certain why some scents inhibit sexual arousal in women, but we did speculate. Maybe cherries induced a memory of taking cherry cough medicine, or the smell of men's cologne may have triggered a memory of a negative dating experience. Regardless, we found that if your goal is to arouse a woman, it is not going to happen with the smell of your cologne.

Perfume Has Its Advantages

This does not mean, however, that perfume is completely useless when it comes to human connection. It just doesn't seem to have a place in romance. We have found that it can play a role in other facets of life where getting along with someone or making a good first impression are important.

Let's say, for example, you are scheduled for a job interview and you need to make a good impression. Well, there are a few strategies you can use to come out on top.

In general, people are primarily narcissists. You can assume that since we like ourselves, we prefer others to be like us. Or, put another way, people who have things in common are likely to get along. This draw toward similarity creates a type of behavior that helps explain the reason (though it's not always a rational one) why one person lands a particular job and the other candidate does not. So it may pay off to look, sound, act, and even smell like the person who is interviewing you.

Our research has found that you don't actually have to be like another person you want to impress as long as you can mirror certain behaviors that can help build compatibility. Some experts on body language say that if you can subtly match certain behaviors, like crossing your legs if the interviewer does, or resting your chin on your hand if the other person does, then the conversation will move toward compatibility.

> Romantic compatibility can be defined as two people who complement one another.

One of the bumps in the road toward "similarity" is that we don't always have the information we need to pull it off. However, based on current information about scents in the workplace, I can offer some advice, although they obviously apply to a limited number of situations. On a job interview, the best-case scenario is for you and the interviewer to wear the same scent. Of course, it is very unlikely that you would have this information, but at least try to find out if you will be interviewed by a man or a woman. Then use this little bit of knowledge to your advantage:

* A man interviewing with a man should wear a spicy odor.

* A woman interviewing with a man should not use a

scent because research suggests that, in the context of an interview, men perceive perfume as a form of female manipulation.

* A woman interviewing with another woman should wear a floral smell, unless she happens to know the specific fragrance the other woman likes. If you show up wearing her perfume, it will appeal to the female interviewer's narcissistic tendency, and there's a greater likelihood that the two of you will get along.

Be forewarned. While this may work in a business and possibly even in a social situation, the same rules do not apply to the compatibility of love. Though sameness appeals to our basic narcissistic essence, being too similar to your mate can lead to trouble. If both partners are aggressive, no-lose competitors, then the friction that results can kill the relationship. Romantic compatibility may be defined as two people who complement each other. It may be that relationships work best if viewed like a jigsaw puzzle and the personalities, with all their quirks, fit. For example, one partner is obsessed with neatness and the other is relatively laissez-faire; or one is outgoing, while the other is more contemplative and needs time alone. These relationships, or any combination of complementary personality traits, usually grow stronger for their differences.

Women Have
Better Noses

The influence of scent can show up in many disguises during a courtship, especially to the noses of women. Women have a better ability to smell than men do, which means they are able to detect flavors in foods that men cannot. This explains, at least in part, why men often prefer more heavily spiced dishes, because they help enhance the taste and, therefore, the pleasure of food.

The gender difference in the ability to smell shows up in other ways, too. For example, alcohol and cigarettes tend to diminish the sense of smell, and men tend to drink more than women. At one time, men were the heavier smokers, although that is not as true today. However, if a woman is dating a man who smokes, she might notice that he is also a heavy cologne user. It's not intentional; more likely, he can't pick up the scent because his smell is dulled by cigarettes.

> There's a reason why men go a little heavy on the cologne.

These differences in the ability to smell can come into play in a relationship in which a man is older than a woman, which is still the norm when choosing life partners. The sense of smell starts to diminish as we age—among men and women alike—so an older man will have a much worse sense of smell than his significantly younger partner. If we were programmed to marry based on equality of the nose, then men would naturally gravitate toward older women!

Thinness Is in the Eye of the . . .

It's common for people to make conscious judgments of others, especially when it comes to sizing up potential relationships with the opposite sex. What you may not realize is that these judgments unconsciously are based on the way the person smells. We have a deeply ingrained response that says, "You are as you smell."

Smell good and you are good; but if you smell bad, that means you are bad. If a man smells bad, almost no matter what positive qualities he has going for him, women will reject him. This is particularly important in our present society where natural odors are eliminated. For the most part, they aren't even considered in terms of what makes a person attractive. In the United States, where running water is taken for granted, many people shower more than once a day. We're so clean, we squeak, so it is impossible for someone's natural good smell to stand out.

This evaluation of a person based on smell is not unlike a

woman's preference for a tall man. Studies demonstrate not only the preference for tall men, but actual rejection of shorter males.

Visual perception of a man's height will influence a woman's desire to go out with him. That probably doesn't come as a big surprise to anyone— male or female. It is also documented that odors can affect this visual perception. For example, when women wear an aroma that smells some- what like mixed floral spicy scent, combined with Old Spice, men perceive them as thinner by an average of 12 pounds.

This same odor, however, had no effect on women's perception of men's weight. There are two possible explanations for this: Maybe women are much better than men at estimating weight, or perhaps men are so easily influenced by a woman's scent that it overpowers their powers of reason.

❙ You can smell thinner!

This is not a recommendation for women to run out and buy a perfume that smells like mixed flowers and spices. These "thinning" scents can't trick all men. For example, some men, such as tailors, were not affected by the aroma. It's possible that tailors, by the skills honed through their profession, are accurate at estimating a woman's weight.

We illustrated this with men working at Six Flags Great America amusement park north of Chicago, where one can participate in a game in which a pitchman guesses weight. If he guesses wrong, the customer wins a teddy bear. If he guesses right, the customer loses the money spent to play the game. Like tailors, the men running this game were much more accurate in their weight assessments, even when women wore the "thinning" mixed flowers and spices scent. That's because these men are systematic in assessing weight, and not just influenced by a woman's overall attractiveness.

We found that the mixed floral-spicy scent is the olfactory equivalent of wearing vertical stripes. In other words, to look thinner, a woman can don a jacket with a vertical line design or add a dab or two of a mixed floral-spicy aroma. Either way, she will appear thinner to her date—unless, of course, he's a pitchman at an amusement park.

Men Are "Ageists"

Just as women reject short men, men reject older women. Not withstanding the movie *Harold and Maude*, men prefer younger women. Like society as a whole, men tend to be "ageists" and appreciate younger women more than older women or, more to the point, they find them more sexually arousing. This could be an innate response from ancient times when youth represented the opportunity to procreate. But remember, we found that the aroma of pink grapefruit can create an illusion that can make men think a woman is, on average, 6 years younger than she actually is. Here, again, we found that the food smell that can trick a man won't trick a woman. Women can sniff grapefruit all day long, but men will still look their age.

Is the Nose Too Important?

There is no question that smell influences our choice in mates, even though we are not cognizant of it. It is not yet fully understood why this is, but the knowledge has led us to discover other related techniques that can help determine the potential for a long-term relationship between two people.

We have found that one can determine a person's personality type by the kinds of foods a person prefers. And, by extension, we can use food preference to play matchmaker.

To this day, people retain their evolutionary instincts to pursue and find a mate to procreate as soon and as often as possible. Unfortunately, the odds that you will find Mr. or Miss Right are against you. However, we found a mechanism that will help you greatly increase your odds. It means stepping across that innate evolutionary path—what some might call our animal instincts—to search in a different way. It allows you to move beyond the immediate drives and view potential partners from the perspective of whom you might get along with over a longer period of time—far longer than the time it takes to reproduce!

4

BREAKFAST ON THE RUN— DATING STYLE

Eggs, fruit, sweets, cereal? **Get a** glimpse of what gets him going in the morning and you'll get a view of his basic outlook on life. You'll also be off to a good start in your search for compatibility.

• • • • •

For some reason, it seems that almost every mother in the world urges her children to eat breakfast—and probably claims it's the most important meal of the day. While it's unclear if this is actually true, breakfast is an important meal for grown-ups playing the mating game.

Although breakfast is not the most common meal shared on a date (at least not early in the relationship), knowing what someone eats for breakfast can tell you a lot about a person's true personality. This is key because figuring out a person's underlying essence is significant to understanding if a person is a match for you.

The choices in the following quiz are not a comprehensive rundown of favorite breakfast foods, but each has consistently shown to be representative of a broad group of food choices that reveal something distinctive about personality. The quiz is deceptively simple and, when viewed in the context of hundreds of possible food choices, demonstrates how a few seemingly minor food preferences offer clues to a person's personality.

BREAKFAST ON THE RUN

So, just for fun, I'd like you to take this quiz. For each of the choices, 1 through 3, select which food you prefer.

1. A) Lemons
   B) Oranges

2. A) Potatoes
   B) Yams

3. A) Grapefruit
   B) Tangerines

This is what the answers reveal:

If you picked "A" in two out of three food choices—lemons, potatoes, or grapefruit—it profiles you as a quiet, reserved, contemplative person who tends to think before you leap. You are the opposite of compulsive.

If you chose "B" in two out of three options—oranges, yams, or tangerines—then you are probably outgoing—a person others might call an extrovert. However, you'd like to enjoy a stable relationship.

WHAT'S YOUR FOOD SIGN?

You Are
What You Eat

This deceptively simple quiz can give you information about someone (in this case yourself), and it is a technique you will use to learn important information about other people's personalities. Here is an example of how you can use this information. Your friend Jim, whom you would describe as reserved, orders grapefruit juice and hash browns as part of his breakfast, two of the choice "A" answers. Compare this to the information above and you'll see that this system has some validity. In other words, Jim shows that we, indeed, "are what we eat."

> Ambitious, independent types go for "serious" cereals, such as Raisin Bran. The less ambitious, take-it-one-day-at-a-time types go for the kid stuff, like Lucky Charms.

Practice making observations like this when you go out for breakfast with friends. You may gain some insight into their basic personality traits or perhaps confirm a certain hunch you have about particular individuals. It's a great way to hone your skills as a food preference–watcher.

In personality typing, we often see a clear distinction between two basic outlooks on life. Some people believe that they are responsible for their own choices and that they essentially control their own destiny. These people fall into a personality type described as having an *internal locus of control.* Put simply, these men and women take the attitude that they are in the "driver's seat." They tend to be ambitious, independent, aggressive, and take control of their own goals. This type of person prefers "serious" cereals, such as Raisin Bran.

Those with an *external locus of control* may look at life in a more fatalistic way. They may shrug their shoulders and say, "Who knows why things happen?" Give them those fun kids' cereals, like Alpha-Bits and Lucky Charms. These are the people who check their horoscopes daily and, while they may not admit it, they often feel as if their fate is not in their hands but is written in "the stars." They may be less ambitious and aggressive, but they tend to maintain traditional values.

Some of the personality traits seem consistent among a group of foods. There is nothing incongruous about a person who is ambitious and responsible being an optimistic self-starter. The same person whose personality is consistent with preferring pancakes and syrup one day may order a specific cereal on another day. For example, those we identify as having an internal locus of control may have boxes of Rice Krispies or Raisin Bran in their kitchen cabinets. These men and women may also grab granola bars for breakfast on the run or as snacks.

WHAT'S YOUR FOOD SIGN?

Do Real Men Like Pink?

∙∙

Example 1

A man is at breakfast and has to choose one of these foods:

> A) Half a pink grapefruit
> B) A doughnut

Based on food surveys that identified some gender-specific food preferences, we found that:

* Men who prefer pink grapefruit for breakfast tend to think about sex most of the time. They are sexually expressive and perhaps even sexually aggressive. From a woman's perspective, these men also may be on the domineering side, and may impulsively jump into intimate relationships.

* Men who order doughnuts for breakfast tend to be sexually reserved. If you're a woman, you may be pleased to know that these men will be interested in more than sex and express curiosity about other areas of your life. Doughnut-loving men also value their friendships with other men and tend to enjoy

doing things in groups, but they are also contemplative, thoughtful types. These men may be a bit afraid
of women, perhaps because they fear rejection.

. . . .

Example 2

**A woman is at breakfast and has to choose one of these
foods:**

A) Banana-nut bread
B) A bowl of cherries

We found that:

* Women who prefer banana-nut bread tend to enjoy
  romantic and sexual fantasies and use them as an
  escape. They are sensitive women who may be considered "seekers" because they enjoy self-discovery
  and are inquisitive. They also enjoy physical contact.

* Women who prefer cherries are more conservative
  and tend to see things in black-and-white, which
  may make them uncompromising and unrealistic
  in relationships.

. . . .

Example 3

Either a man or woman is at breakfast and has a choice among:

> A) Grapes
> B) Plums
> C) Prunes

We found that:

* Choosing grapes or plums suggests they are contemplative, quiet, introverts who often turn to solitary activities. Those who choose prunes are extroverted. They tend to be outgoing and enjoy participating in activities that include other people. Since they like social settings, you are likely to find them working in large offices. They prefer shopping at malls rather than small boutiques or specialty stores.

. . . .

Fruit-lovers in general tend to be optimistic, pleasant, and good at friendships. These are good qualities in a mate. Other differences can be found in the types of fruit people enjoy. The grapes-plums-prunes exercise is one example. Another is seen in our ice cream studies (see Chapter 9) of fruit-flavored choices.

For example, men who favor strawberry tend to be insecure in many aspects of their lives, including the bedroom. They are easily hurt and often feel inadequate, but like to be dominated. They take even minor criticism as serious remarks. Women should keep in mind that just because a date prefers strawberries and may be insecure, he may also be a loyal friend and an optimistic partner.

Butter pecan ice cream–lovers will also order pecan rolls for breakfast. This is not indicative of an adventurous sort, but it may not matter much because these men tend to be loyal and true. Straying is not in their nature. Unfortunately, women tend to eventually get bored with them.

One day, we may know what ordering a pumpkin muffin or a poppy-seed bagel or walnut coffeecake for breakfast says about a personality. Until that time, we can speak only in generalizations. But a profile exists of people who prefer pastries for breakfast. They are contemplative and thoughtful, sexually reserved, and probably fear rejection.

Fruit-lovers in general are optimistic and pleasant and make good friends.

When I give you examples of sample meals, you'll note that I sometimes link the strawberry or prune or pecan personality with that flavor or type of pastry. I think it's logical to cross certain flavor preferences from one food to another, but always remember that these preferences are

Men, Women, and Control

. . . .

The word "control" is a loaded word, especially when it comes to the interplay between male and female. Control issues show up as differences between men and women, but they are tangential to the basic orientation of the *locus of control.*

Shaving is a good example, because our research has found that women and men have different attitudes about their razor blades. First, men tend to change their razor blade every day or two, whereas women will keep the same razor blade for months. Perhaps this is because when men shave and cut themselves, they blame the blade, but when women shave and cut themselves, they perceive that they slipped. Men tend to blame external factors, whereas women tend to internalize this blame.

This kind of blaming behavior shows up in other ways, too. In households across the country, there are two very different versions of the same simple question: "Where are my keys?"

Men: Where did *you* put my keys?

Women: Where did *I* leave my keys?

This type of interaction can lead to all kinds of "What do you mean?" and "Don't blame me" responses while men and women try to figure each other out.

only clues to help us form impressions about individual personalities. These clues are important in solving the mystery of the hidden personality.

The Secrets
Behind the
"S" Words

Clearly, it is not possible to mate personality traits with every imaginable food. Nor is it necessary. We can lump certain foods into broader categories of tastes. You'll see what I mean by taking this test. So, without overthinking the issue, which taste do you prefer?

> A) Sour
> B) Salty
> C) Sweet
> D) Spicy

A preference for one of the four tastes automatically offers hints into certain personality traits. Over time, you will be able to fit your potential partner into one of these general categories.

* **Sour:** Those who prefer sour foods are intensely loyal, particularly because tart or sour is not inherently pleasant. These individuals will run from confrontation, so you won't have many fights. If you want a commitment that lasts, regardless of its quality, then

watch for the sour-lovers. These individuals will enjoy the good relationships, but endure the bad ones.

* **Salty:** If you notice the salt shaker is used a lot at the table, then there's something primal about this person's drives. The first taste any of us ever have is the salty amniotic fluid in our mother's womb, and a craving for salt is like being pulled back to safety and security, while at the same time looking for raw, primal sexuality.

* **Sweet:** Those who look for the sweet items on the menu like to feel special, and they treat others that way, too. You might say that they enjoy life's rewards—desserts—and they aren't afraid to indulge. These individuals have few regrets and are the pure hedonists among us.

* **Spicy:** People who order spicy dishes are always on the prowl for a "charge." They're thrill-seekers and need stimulation. In fact, spicy foods irritate the trigeminal nerve in the face, which is why our eyes water when we peel an onion. People who choose these "irritating" foods will probably always seek the next adventure, and those who live with them better be prepared for their partner's restless energy.

Practice Session:
What's on
the Menu

* **Grapefruit, a pecan roll, a cheese omelet, and coffee with cream** . . . then he or she is likely quiet and thoughtful, probably a detail-oriented person who follows the rules (those who like butter pecan ice cream tend to follow all the rules) and likes to be secure. They tend to enjoy the good things in life, though, even if they consider that indulgent.

* **Pancakes, a fruit cup, and black coffee** . . . then he or she likes to be in control and, in general, is an optimistic person who goes after ambitious goals. This person enjoys planning ahead, but tends to avoid physical risks. These individuals might prefer to attend a business seminar rather than spend the same money on skydiving lessons.

WHAT'S YOUR FOOD SIGN?

* **Black coffee and a banana muffin . . .** then she enjoys sexual fantasy. She aggressively pursues her goals, and if one of them is a relationship, then watch out. She's looking for a partner and may have read all the books about finding one. She also has the propensity to take off for a weekend retreat or seminar where she'll learn journaling or meditation.

How Do You Like Your Eggs?

This is a normal question, so use it to your advantage. We don't have a great deal of specific information on egg-lovers, but we do know something about people who like their eggs scrambled: They are risk-takers.

Cheese omelet–lovers are just the opposite. They are so risk-adverse that they may even choose a career that is physically secure and safe, like accounting or banking.

On the other hand, if you are out to breakfast with someone who orders scrambled eggs spiced up with peppers and onions, then you may be with a person who takes the idea of risk to the extreme. These are fire fighters and people in love with the idea of being an astronaut or racecar driver.

This applies to men and women alike.

* **A cherry sweet roll and a chai latte** . . . then she is conservative and pessimistic, perhaps even rigid. At times she is anxious and easily annoyed.

* **A strawberry sweet roll and hot chocolate** . . . then he tends to be intolerant about any criticism. He sees such criticism as a threat and it makes him feel less secure. Tending to be sexually insecure, he is a romantic idealist and may also be quite dependent.

* **A doughnut and scrambled eggs with peppers and onions** . . . then he may be a sexually reserved risk-take, who may also be shy around women, even a bit afraid of them, because of his underlying fear of rejection. In other words, he may sign up for skydiving, but has to work up courage to ask a woman out on a date. He will be loyal, though, and know how to be a good friend.

Food for
Thought

There are no right or wrong personalities, so what you observe or view as positive or perhaps not-so-pleasing traits are subjective and apply only to your personal preference. If you like the charming risk-taker, but that drive for adventure is a bit much for you, introduce him to your friend who likes to hang around with people who live a little dangerously. They could be made for each other!

5

LET'S MEET FOR COFFEE— OR HOW ABOUT A COLD DRINK?

Will your relationship be hot or cold? Take your potential mate on a café date to test your compatibility.

• • • • •

The suggestion to "meet for coffee" isn't what it used to be. Today, you're more likely to hear, "Let's meet for latte." Long gone are the days when coffee preference was defined with the simple question: "Cream and sugar?"

Though those days may be gone, coffee is more popular than ever. Globally, two out of every three people routinely drink coffee in its various forms—latte, cappuccino, Frappucino, just to name a few—to the tune of four *billion* cups a day. After water, coffee is the most-consumed beverage in the world.

What Is It
About Coffee,
Anyway?

A host of possible reasons exist to explain the intense and nearly universal thirst for coffee. One is its caffeine content and its ability to act as a social lubricant of sorts, much like alcohol. Most people report that they enjoy coffee for its taste, yet ironically they describe this "alluring" taste as being "burnt," "bitter," and "rank" on one extreme, to being "delicate," "mild," and "smooth" on the other extreme. This may be because coffee actually has a bitter taste, but it can be sweet as well.

Clearly, no one can pinpoint, as we can with ice cream or even burgers, why this particular liquid in all its variations has such special and worldwide appeal. But in his 1982 book, *Memoir for Forgetfulness,* Palestinian poet Mahmoud Darwish said this about coffee: "There is nothing one could call the taste of coffee; it is not a concept, a concrete object, a thing in itself. Everyone has his own 'coffee,' so idiosyncratic that I can judge a man, sense his inner elegance, by the kind of coffee he serves."

Today, the type of coffee someone prefers rivals fashion when it comes to making a social statement.

We've studied coffee at a unique time in its history; never has there been so much choice in coffee flavors, blends, and varieties. It's hard to keep pace with the ever-expanding options. Today coffee and, to a lesser extent, tea are as important a social statement as fashion, music, and movies.

The Trend
Toward
Choice

Coffee is just another example of the trend away from simplicity. Think of ice cream when the selection was limited to just a dozen or so flavors. Now we see flavors in the hundreds. Soft drinks are following suit. Not that long ago, Coke was just Coke or Diet Coke. The word itself defined the taste. Then came decaffeinated and, almost overnight, or so it seemed, we had vanilla, lemon, and lime-flavored Coke. And additional flavors in other popular soft drinks abound, too.

This proliferation of flavor choices in all foods makes a lot of sense because it shows that our society is designed to cater to a diverse population. In an affluent country of almost 300 million, it's logical that companies would devote great resources to satisfy individual personalities and changes in taste that result from changing demographic trends. For example, because our population is aging, we will see a corresponding change in the ability to taste and smell, so test marketers might well produce foods designed to deliver more intense smells and tastes.

> The increasing array of choices in all consumer items offers the opportunity for individual expression.

Unlimited choices in so many areas of everyday life are marketed through the appeal of expressing our individual personalities. This applies to perfume, chocolate, soft drinks, clothing, shoes, houses, and yes, even coffee. On a psychological level, we are given the impression that our food preferences can be as unique as our handwriting. It's all part of "eating who we are."

> In a sense, coffee is
> like a glue that holds
> us together socially.

The era in which variety is king may appeal to many people, but we're losing a component of society that in the past provided a sense of bonding. At one time, huge numbers of people watched the last episode of *All in the Family*, *Hill Street Blues*, *M.A.S.H.*, or *Seinfeld*. Trends in television viewing and 300-plus channels have polarized the population. In a household of four, everyone can be in a different room watching a different show.

The move toward multiple choices is leading to polarization in our society. The trend toward greater individual choice in virtually everything may put us at risk for denying some basic human needs and even instincts. For example, the desire to share food indicates our basic drive to belong, so when tens of millions of households sit down to eat the same kinds of food for Thanksgiving dinner, we're expressing a cultural bond as well as a family one.

This discussion may seem unrelated to coffee, but it isn't. On one level, coffee and, to some extent, tea have served as a kind of "glue" that holds us together. We used to drink it in

89

cups that have saucers and in homes and diners and company cafeterias and in rooms designated as "coffee rooms" in factories and offices. Now we sip coffee from carryout cups or mugs and we pay up to several dollars (without refills!) for a coffee drink that might bear little or no resemblance to what the person across from us or in the next office may be drinking. On the other hand, we gravitate toward the atmosphere that brings us together to share coffee, from the retirees who congregate to talk over a cup of coffee each morning at the local diner to the bookstore cafés where book-browsers lounge in a communal atmosphere to read and relax. The commonality of the coffee experience is one of our cultural glues.

The Enigma of the Taste

Coffee's value as a potentially pleasant substance—the hedonic value—is determined by its smell and taste, but those factors don't fully explain its lure. Almost everyone agrees that coffee has a bitter taste, which some people mask with sugar and milk. Even its ardent supporters will admit that it has no nutritional value and certainly isn't listed in one of the food groups. It contains the stimulant caffeine, which helps energize us and get us through bouts of fatigue during the course of a day. Some see this as positive and others view it as negative, because when coffee acts as a stimulate it can put people on edge and keep them awake at night. As an alternative, they turn to the decaffeinated varieties rather than forgo the pleasure of this "taste."

> There is more to our
> attraction to coffee than its
> bitter taste—much more.

Most likely, the initial lure toward drinking coffee in our society is its symbolic value as a "grownup" substance. Many associate drinking coffee with one of their first adult activities, and it may even forge a bond between the generations. Some people remember the feeling of belonging when they "came of age" and were allowed to share after-dinner coffee with their parents or older siblings. With idealized memories like that, it's no wonder the desire for coffee remains stable for life. Since coffee may be among the first odors we are exposed to, our positive response to its aroma may be rooted in nostalgia. It may sound ridiculous, but every cup of coffee may be an unconscious attempt to re-create this idealized past, which is the essence of gustatory-evoked nostalgia.

Whatever the reason, no one drinks coffee for sensory reasons alone. In fact, it could be said that, like chili peppers (which actually can damage the taste buds), we consume coffee despite its bitter taste. It's much more likely that the coffee image—that is, its positive associations and the perception of its desirability—is what attracts us to coffee.

Once people decide they like coffee and they begin to consume it regularly, they often will crave it. Cravings for coffee may be based on internal biological demands or psychological factors. For example, if you become deficient in salt, then you may crave salty foods. Psychologically, we may crave coffee as a method to reduce anxiety or prepare emotionally for the day. It may become a consistent, habitual way of shifting a mood.

Coffee—
Black, Please

The place you most likely will find people sipping plain old coffee—black or with cream and sugar—is at breakfast or after a meal. In fact, you can score an instant hit in personality assessment if you spy someone drinking coffee "straight." We've found that those who drink black coffee tend to have an internal locus of control—meaning they are responsible, ambitious, independent, and aggressive. This same personality profile matches those who generally like cereal, too. (People who order hot chocolate for breakfast are the opposite of black coffee drinkers in many ways, even tending toward dependency. They tend to be romantic to the point where they are no longer realistic about their partners.)

We also were able to match personality types for those who prefer some of the more exotic choices, concoctions that would have been virtually unknown in the United States a few years ago.

....

* **Chai latte** . . . he or she may be a stressed-out, cranky type, probably pessimistic and anxious. This person tends to be shy and on the stubborn side.

* **Gingerbread latte** . . . this person enjoys power and feels special. This person seeks the best and may be easily irritated.

* **Iced mocha** . . . he or she is lively, dramatic, seductive, and flirtatious. This person may also be unconcerned about the future.

* **Mocha-flavored coffee** . . . these people seek comfort in others, though they may be unreliable. Look for signs of underlying depression.

* **Café au lait** . . . he or she likes tradition, is not particularly ambitious, and may even be superstitious.

Obviously, these are very different personality types. When we look at these opposites, can we say for sure that they wouldn't be compatible? Not necessarily. The hot chocolate-lover may admire the black coffee-drinker's independence, and some of his or her romantic nature may rub off on the more-driven coffee-drinker.

A Reading at the Café

With so many choices, we decided to do our research on the popular iced, flavored coffees called Frappuccinos. A total of 800 volunteers, mostly female, all took the series of psychological tests mentioned elsewhere in this book. We then asked them to choose their favorites among three ice-blended beverages: coffee-based, cream-based, and tea/fruit-based. We then correlated personality characteristics as follows:

Coffee-based Frappucino: These individuals are aggressive, energetic self-starters who are both independent and ambitious. They're optimists who also tend to overcommit, although they're lively and passionate in everything they do. While logically oriented in their relationships, when it comes to romance, they're also likely to be dramatic, seductive, and flirtatious.

Cream-based Frappuccino: We could describe these individuals as unrealistic idealists who are easily suggestible. They are hopeless romantics prone to flights of romantic fantasy. They're dependent types that are at their best when they're in a close, secure relationship. They are intuitive and tend to be impulsive. By nature, they are expressive and often fall into a state of depression. On the other hand, they are colorful risk-takers who are gregarious, crave novelty, and are easily bored by the usual routine.

Tea/fruit-based Frappucino: These individuals are shy, irritable, and stubborn. These pessimists often feel insecure and inadequate. Hypersensitive to criticism, they may appear anxious and highly stressed. While they tend to be loners, they are loyal team players who are good at supporting group efforts. These men and women, who would rather follow than lead, approach work and social situations in a serious and thoughtful way.

I'll Take
Iced Tea
Instead

With coffee drinking at an all-time high and a central theme for social gathering, you'd think everyone would be in on the trend. There are some people who just never acquire the taste for coffee and prefer milder teas or sweetened drinks. If you or the person you are dating fall in this camp, here is a quiz that will give you some personality clues.

Once again, simply pick one favorite among the following choices:

A) Lemonade
B) Pink lemonade
C) Iced tea with lemon
D) Cool raspberry iced tea
E) Decaffeinated plain iced tea
F) Green tea with peach

Neither lemonade nor iced tea has the kind of "mystique" that coffee has but both drinks are noteworthy in their own ways. Lemonade has an element of nostalgia and may remind you of your childhood and carefree times. Iced tea is, in some ways, an adult version of lemonade. We associate it with summer, and in some parts of the country, the designation "sweet tea" is understood by everyone to mean sweetened iced tea. Unlike reaching for a soft drink, lemonade and iced tea must be prepared, which moves them into the "sweet treat" category.

Our research of 441 people, mostly women, found no runaway favorite. Plain old lemonade was most preferred at 25

percent, followed by: pink lemonade, 15 percent; iced tea with lemon, 18 percent; cool raspberry iced tea, 16 percent; decaffeinated iced tea, 14 percent; green tea with peach, 12 percent. Here is what our personality assessment showed.

LEMONADE-LOVERS ARE:

* **Easy going and avoid conflict.** They will agree with things they think are wrong rather than create disagreement or confrontation.

* **Loyal.** This applies to their jobs and their relationships.

* **Always faithful.** When they commit themselves romantically, it is for life. They will (almost) never stray.

Those who prefer lemonade are most romantically compatible with others who also prefer lemonade.

PINK LEMONADE-LOVERS ARE:

* **Private people.** They enjoy their privacy and are most creative when secluded from the day-to-day interruptions of work and social frustration.

* **Often self-absorbed.** They can become so fascinated with their work or hobbies that they may seem rude.

* **Creative.** Pink lemonade-lovers are the inventors/ mad scientist types like we saw in the movie Back to the Future.

Those who prefer pink lemonade are most romantically compatible with those who prefer iced tea with lemon.

ICED TEA WITH LEMON-LOVERS ARE:

* **Perfectionists.** They are devoted to work and are ideal employees. They set high standards for themselves and others.

* **Take-charge types.** These are orderly individuals who take charge of tasks without procrastinating.

* **Reserved in all they do.** They are ethical, fiscally conservative, and logical, as opposed to intuitively orientated.

* **Romantically shy.** They often are sexually shy or inhibited.

Those who prefer iced tea with lemon are most romantically compatible either with others who also prefer iced tea with lemon, or those who prefer lemonade.

WHAT'S YOUR FOOD SIGN?

* **Success-oriented.** These men and women are day-dreamers who will go on to achieve success and enjoy the trimmings of success.

* **A bit spoiled.** Because they are used to being waited on, they can, from a distance, come across as being arrogant. However, up close, you will find them to be rather vulnerable and sensitive to the criticisms of others.

* **Comfortable in the limelight.** They are the leaders in politics and business, and they are used to having things their way.

Those who like cool raspberry are best off remaining single. Should you end up with one, be prepared to play the role of "second fiddle."

* **Colorful and impulsive.** They live somewhat chaotic lives and are always on the go. They can make a life-time decision quickly, but often live to regret it.

* **Social butterflies.** They make a strong impression on those around them, and they thrive in the company of others.

Decaffeinated iced tea–lovers are most romantically compatible with other decaffeinated iced tea–lovers.

**GREEN TEA WITH
PEACH–**LOVERS ARE:

* **Outgoing.** These men and women adore being the center of attention.

* **Flirtatious.** They are extroverts who love to act seductive and dramatic.

* **Happy playing the field.** They tend to become romantically involved quickly, but tire of relationships easily—including friends. They have trouble keeping long-term commitments.

Green tea with peach–lovers are most romantically compatible with those who prefer lemonade or decaffeinated iced tea.

So, You're Out on a Date . . .

Coffee is a common interest among so many people, and it is a good dating activity that doesn't require an investment of too much money or time. A café also provides the opportunity for conversation without the distraction of a meal. Here are some observations you should

make in collecting your food clues. Use these small clues to open up a conversation about the new world of coffees. You may hear your date admit that he's a creature of habit, and always orders the same coffee Frap, or she'll tell you that no matter what's on the menu, she always orders black coffee anyway.

* Does your date order right away?

* Does your date study the menu and talk about the dilemma of choice?

* Does your date study the menu, but end up with black coffee anyway?

* Does you date order a drink that has more cream than coffee?

So, it's a hot afternoon and you find yourself in a café or at a refreshment stand in a park. Here is an easy, non-threatening way to suggest stopping for a glass of lemonade or iced tea.

* **If your date orders plain decaf iced tea, you might ask if he or she has tried the newer flavors.** If the answer is no, try to find out why. Some people won't try any new foods. Your date may simply say, "I don't bother with those flavor fads." Or, if the answer is yes, you might hear, "Oh sure. I always try new things, but in this case, I like the plain tea better." Both answers provide clues and neither are all bad. Maybe you're a lemonade-lover through and through and your date orders pink lemonade. Try asking your date questions about how she spends her private time. Ask, "What are your hobbies?" If she tells you that she enjoys stargazing and hobbies that are done alone, then you have confirmation of one of the pink lemonade–lover's personality traits. You may not mind this person's need to be alone.

* **Try a guessing game.** If your date is flirtatious and dramatic, you could say, "Let me guess, you'll choose that peach-flavored green tea." See what your date's reaction is. Even if that choice isn't on the menu, this dramatic type of person may talk about having a shelf of flavored teas at home.

WHAT'S YOUR FOOD SIGN?

* **Don't forget to do a "compatibility check" with your own preference.** If you're both squeezing lemons into plain tea, you two orderly conservatives may just be a match!

You won't learn the whole range of a person's food preferences based on one date over tea or coffee. But because coffee is so universal, you will be able to collect a lot of clues by making some of the suggested observations. So, keep an eye on what your date orders when you go out for coffee or on hot days at the beach. You may be surprised what you can learn in a short time.

6

THE LUNCH DATE: THE NATURAL WAY TO GET SOCIAL

There is something special about a lunch date that makes getting to know you so easy.

• • • • •

Lunch makes an ideal first-date meal. It's a bigger commitment than meeting for coffee, but it's safer than an open-ended dinner date. Lunch usually has a timeframe, so if things are not going well, there's a built-in escape—*got to get back to the office!* Whether your lunch date ends up rivaling the speed of a fast-food stop or ends up lingering on into dinnertime, the midday meal can be a great getting-to-know-you event.

From a social/cultural perspective, lunch is of prime importance. In the business world, lunch is the venue for impressing important clients, announcing new products, discussing strategy, and sealing a deal. Research has demonstrated that the presence of food can alter attitudes of the diners. If you introduce food to a lively political discussion, for example, people are more likely to agree than if these same points were discussed in a setting without food. This research may validate observations you have made on your own.

There's something about the smell of food itself and the ceremony of sharing a meal that influence a sense of hospitality and acceptance among people. We

even tend to eat more in a group setting. Since most people feel good around food, it helps people get to know each other and like each other better and hence, they are more open to ideas, even ideas they wouldn't normally agree with.

Since the presence of food provides an emotional lift, it's easy to see why lunches have become the place for social and business networking. The important point to remember is that in any interaction where persuasion is an element—be it politics, business, or dating—it's advantageous to make sure that there is some food around. Not only will you and your lunch date tend to see eye-to-eye on more topics of conversation, you'll find each other more agreeable as well.

> The smell of food can influence how we feel and the way we think.

We don't know the exact mechanism that explains why food makes us feel more comfortable and less intimidated, but myriad research suggests that the smell of food can influence both how we feel and how we think.

Getting To
Know You

I hope some of this "lunch talk" helps convince you that having lunch with someone you are interested in is a smart idea. Once done, you can use some of these strategies to help you *really* get to know who are dating. After you are settled in and are looking at the menu, casually ask the question: "What looks good to you?" It is an important question because it will give you a valuable clue to your date's personality type.

* If your date frowns and says, "Well, I see one or two possibilities," when the menu has dozens of items, it's likely you're having lunch with a person who tends to be pessimistic, and sees the proverbial glass as half-full.

* If she sighs happily and says, "Hmm ... so many choices," then it's likely you're dealing with an optimist.

* But, if he says "Everything!" then you can bet that the Pollyanna good cheer indicates that you are with a person who sees the world through rose-colored glasses—and this could be hard to take by the third or fourth date. Or, you could be dating someone who has an omnivorous approach to not only food but to life overall.

A Different
Kind of Date

Clearly, many of the same foods you could order for lunch are foods you'd find on a dinner menu as well, so I've divided them somewhat arbitrarily. Before you see how to match food choices to personality traits, I'd like you to take this short quiz.

Which do you prefer from the following choices?

1. A) Chili
   B) Hamburger

2. A) Tacos
   B) Pancakes with syrup

3. A) Grey Poupon mustard
   B) Tangerines

4. A) Café mocha
   B) Café latte

Before I reveal the answers, here are some examples of how specific choices your date makes are clues to his or her true personality. Feel free to take the quiz yourself.

1. **Which of these two food groups do you prefer?**

     A) Oranges, bananas, and grapes
     B) Eggplant, corn, and tomatoes

2. **Which of the following similar foods do you prefer more? (You must choose one of each pair.)**

     A) Applesauce
     B) A fresh apple

     A) Pineapple chunks
     B) Pineapple glaze

     A) Creamed corn
     B) Corn on the cob

3. **Do you like (circle all the choices you like):**

     A) Bananas
     B) Broiled fish
     C) Fruit
     D) Honey
     E) Tapioca
     F) Nuts
     G) Hot curry

WHAT'S YOUR FOOD SIGN?

4. Do you like spicy pickles?

     A) Yes
     B) No

5. Which do you prefer?

     A) Green olives or black olives
     B) Pecans or almonds
     C) Pickles or cucumbers

WHAT THE ANSWERS MEAN ABOUT YOU—AND YOUR LUNCH DATE

Remember the observations you make will give you important clues to a person's true personality. A single insight will not give you a definitive profile.

Question 1: Fruit Versus Vegetables

* Individuals who chose the fruits over the vegetables are most likely strong-minded and ambitious. They are probably natural leaders in the positive sense, but those of us who don't like being led might call them dominant or aggressive.

* Those who chose the vegetables are likely to be introspective and sensitive to the needs of others. They typically weigh all the alternatives before making a choice.

How to Interpret This Information
On your lunch date, observe how your date selects her food. Choosing a fruit salad makes it easy, but notice if she selects chicken or tuna salad with fruit. Observe if your date leans toward selections in which vegetables dominate.

Question 2: Fruit Styles

Those who select "A" for at least two of the choices tend to be passive and easy-going. These individuals probably make agreeable lunch dates, and if a problem arises, say with bad service, they will try to solve it without making a scene. If the answer is "B" for at least two of the choices, you are likely eating with a person who won't take no for an answer. (This means that you'll always be seated at the better tables!) His dedication to work may impress you, but be prepared for a partner who plays hard and may work long hours, too.

How to Interpret This Information
These particular items may not be on a typical lunch menu, but notice how your date talks about the items on the menu. This may require some prodding on your part. For example, if there is no ham but you see chicken with some sort of fruit

glaze or sauce, you might ask, "So, what do you think about the chicken?" Every small glimpse into food preference is a clue to personality.

Question 3: Picking Favorites

This question hints at a person's underlying optimism and pessimism. Someone who likes five or more of the listed foods is a natural optimist but may view life through very rose-colored glasses. This is also a person who is good to work with and someone who values friends. But if a person dislikes five or more of those foods, it is a characteristic of a suspicious pessimist who may not trust others.

How to Interpret This Information:
The answer to this question initially will give you more insight into yourself than the other person, at least for the first couple of dates. However, over time, if you notice that he hates fish and never eats bananas and avoids fruit most of the time, or you notice that she snacks on the peanuts and puts honey in her hot tea and orders broiled fish with a fruit chutney, then you are starting to collect data that will help lead you to discovering a person's underlying personality.

Question 4: Pickles—Or Not

This question measures optimism and pessimism, too. If you like spicy pickles, you tend to be pessimistic. If not, you tend to be optimistic.

How to Interpret This Information:

The pickle is easy for a lunchtime get-together because most lunch menus offer sandwiches in which a pickle is served. If you don't have your answer after a few dates, go to a deli where you get a choice of pickles to go with a sandwich.

If your lunch date orders spicy pickles, pay close attention to your lunchtime conversation. Do her comments have an edge of doom and gloom? Some people wear their pessimism on their sleeve, so to speak, and some hide it. Though we tend to think it's better to be optimistic, there is a fine line between the genuine mindset and a person who has been trained to act cheerful and upbeat at all times.

Question 5: The Odd Mix

It is difficult to try to explain why the answers to this assortment of foods fall into the categories they do. Regardless, the results correlate with other findings linked to personality assessments. That said, if two or more choices are "A," this person tends to be assertive in his or her relationships and is enthusiastic about everything. Although anxious at times, this is a decisive and resilient person who is prone to act rather than react to life's dilemmas.

If two or more selections are "B," this suggests someone who tends to take responsibility for his own actions and is a self-confident natural leader.

So, Was It
Chili or
Pancakes?

Let's go back to the original question I asked you to answer about yourself on page 109. It's kind of a trick question because it has nothing to do with your personality in particular. Rather it is designed to give you a preliminary glimpse at your olfactory acuity—that is, how well you are able to detect and identify odors.

If you chose "A" at least three times, you prefer spicy foods, which may indicate an impaired or at least slightly diminished sense of smell. People with diminishing smell unconsciously move toward hot, spicy dishes. These men and women may have a tendency to underlying depression, and they may act irritable at times. They are the type of person who will speak up if they think they aren't being treated well enough in a restaurant.

If you chose "B" at least three times, it may indicate that your sense of smell is within the normal range, so you don't need to seek the stimulation of spicy foods.

The spicy versus bland issue offers a few clues into personality, too, and it is one of the most basic findings in food and personality studies. For example, if we sense that we're missing something inherent in our character, we may seek stimulation from foods and smells as well as from other people. On the other hand, if we tend to feel complete in ourselves, we may choose more bland smells and tastes.

Is Your Taste Off?

Take notice if your taste in food begins to change. If you notice that you are starting to gravitate toward spicy foods or adding extra spice to foods you cook, it may be that your sense of smell is diminishing, and therefore, your sense of taste is diminishing, too.

However, this is primarily a health issue, and your underlying personality remains unchanged. Your change in food preferences could be due to the aging process, which in itself causes loss of smell. It's also possible that medications, vitamin deficiencies, and numerous medical conditions may be causing your loss of the ability to smell. I suggest you talk with your physician to try to determine the reason your sense of smell is changing.

Please Pass
the Salt

To get some quick-and-easy insight into your date's basic personality traits, observe his or her use of salt. But before you begin watching other people, take another short quiz.

Which do you prefer?

A) Salty chicken soup
B) Chicken soup prepared
   with little or no salt

Theories about a "salt" personality don't necessarily agree. Some studies suggest that salt-lovers seek outside stimulation and tend to be extroverts, but others have described a "salt personality" called tough poise. A standardized personality test called Cattell's 16 Personality Factors defines tough poise as a decisive and resilient personality that tends to act quickly, often without sufficient consideration.

One theory holds that salt-lovers tune out nutritional advice about limiting salt intake. In this theory, people who don't add salt at the table or when they cook may be worry warts who probably take every health warning seriously. They rarely act on impulse. Our own research offers different insights into the "salt" personality:

If you prefer salty chicken soup, you have an external locus of control, and you may not believe that you control your own destiny. According to this theory, you probably check your horoscope to find out what kind of day you'll have, and rather than making up your own mind, you might follow the crowd when it comes to ideas and opinions. It's possible that rather than having the characteristics of tough poise, you don't watch your salt intake because you don't believe you control your health anyway.

If you chose chicken soup with little or no salt, it's likely that you live as if you're in the driver's seat. This is characteristic of the internal locus of control—these are men and women who go after their goals and will take on leadership roles. You may not use salt because you believe that your health is largely in your own control.

Health Food—
A Link to Personality?

You can tell a lot about an individual by his or her attitude toward food. For example, you probably know individuals who are obsessed about what they eat because they are convinced that certain foods ruin their health and that other foods guarantee youth and vitality.

> Health-food nuts could
> be taking life a little
> too seriously.

These individuals seldom base their beliefs about the "good foods" and "bad foods" on scientific evidence. On personality tests, we find that they tend to be rigid. When people label certain foods as promoting ill-health, they probably tend to fear these foods.

—The reason we have the freedom—we could call it an opportunity—to make so many value judgments about food is because there is so much of it around.

What's Up
with Cheese?

Cheese in various forms has been available for about 8,000 years, so you could say there is nothing new about cheese—except for the variety of shapes in which it is packaged and sold. Probably only the youngest of those on the dating circuit are aware of the wide variety of cheese shapes we can pop in our mouths. Cheese cut into cubes, slices, and shreds are conventional to an older generation. Today's individuals have more choices, including cheese in the shape of sunbursts, stars, and moons.

This observation led us to explore the question: Given the same composition, taste, and cost, would choosing sunbursts over shreds or slices over stars tell us anything about personality? It also begs a second question: What does a willingness to venture into the new world of cheese shapes have to say about a person?

This might strike you as frivolous until you seriously consider these questions. These are the kinds of questions marketers and manufacturers consider in the process of introducing a new food to the public. Internal and external factors come into play in an individual's decision to even try something new.

> There's an easy way to find out if your date has a spirit of adventure.

In an earlier chapter, I mentioned neophobia, the fear of new things. This exists in both humans and animals. It makes sense to be cautious about consuming unknown things, because we literally don't know if a particular leaf, berry, or animal is toxic. For some peo-

ple, even a new shape—like the cheese—could, on an unconscious level, flash a warning sign.

Counterbalancing a natural fear of new foods is the innate need to search for, and ingest, new and different things, including foods. We call this desire for new food venturesomeness. In the course of growing up, these two innate needs become integrated.

Food
Expectations

Expectation plays a big role in our attraction or aversion to food and odors. We expect tomatoes to be red. Peanut butter should be the color of peanuts. So, for many older people, cheese should be served in cubes or slices—the ways their parents served it to them. Not only do the old standard shapes feel safe, they are what is expected.

The new green or purple ketchup makes the older consumer uneasy—and it may even kill appetite for ketchup. Odd as it sounds, the newer cheese shapes can have the same effect on older people because the physical appearance of the cheese does not meet the preconceived notion of the right forms in which cheese is sold. But, the younger generation (and the young at heart) doesn't have this bias; they are generally more free-spirited, imaginative, and playful with food. The younger generation is more inclined to embrace these shapes, the same way they willingly try other foods that are different or novel—peanut butter and jelly in the same jar, bubble gum ice cream, and gummy candies shaped like bears or worms.

The spirit of adventure in food, however, only goes so far. Almost no one, including small children, can overcome the cultural barrier that eating certain animals is wrong. We could hear some news report that monkey liver is good for our health, but virtually no one would care. In mainstream culture in the United States, we can't even think about ingesting such a food—and we don't even call it a food, of course. No matter what other values unite a society, these shared concepts of the appropriateness of foods may be the most defining characteristic of a culture.

121

You Eat
What You
Are

To better understand the link between food choices and personality traits, the aphorism, "you are what you eat," should be reversed to "you eat what you are." The belief that we do become what we eat is a cross-cultural phenomenon that can be found not only among the cannibals of New Guinea, but even in the U.S., on college campuses, where undergraduates in one study subscribed to the notion that those who eat boar are more boarlike and those eat turtle possess "turtlesque" traits.

> Making food choices
> is all about sensory
> experience.

If you can take this theory and apply it to the cheese example, then the unconscious motivation to prefer cheese in the shapes of stars and moons may indicate an underlying desire to become heavenly, pure, and celestial. Perhaps the sunburst reinforces the desire to be optimistic and experience happy-go-lucky emotions. The old-fashioned cubes and slices could represent a perfectionistic, rigid personality. Or those who prefer shredded cheese have a sadistic, masochistic, aggressive streak. Choices about all kinds of sensory experiences—what we like to look at, listen to, smell, and touch—offer clues to a person's underlying personality.

What's Your
Cheese Shape?

We performed a study to answer this question. A total of 647 men and women volunteered and went through all the personality tests that we used in all our research. The majority of people, 57 percent, preferred their cheese in cubes. The remaining preferences were: stars and moons, 17 percent; slices, 12 percent; shreds, 12 percent; and sunbursts, 4 percent. When we measured their preferences against the results of their personality tests, specific personality types emerged.

CUBE-LOVERS ARE:

* **Conscientious and detail-oriented perfectionists.** They can be so devoted to work that they have trouble finding the time to relax and spend quality time with the family.

* **Happiest when they control their environment.** They try to avoid unexpected or nontraditional experiences whenever possible, which is why they hesitate to forge new territory.

* **Xenophobic.** When traveling to new places (even foreign countries), they tend to choose McDonald's

or a Holiday Inn or Hilton rather than explore the local restaurants and hotels.

* **Traditionalists when it comes to food choices.** Apparently, a reluctance to experiment extends into food choices, for most cube-lovers prefer simpler, more traditional American cuisine to spicier, bolder flavors.

* **Conservative when it comes to fashion.** They aren't bold with colors and are more concerned with looking professional and sensible than fashionable.

But as a partner . . .

Cube-lovers can be cautious and restrained when meeting new people, but once they trust you, they are loyal. Depending on where they live and how old they are, their hobbies can include many activities, but they generally prefer quieter pastimes such as reading, watching movies, and being around their family and friends—at least when they can find the time! Learning to take a few moments out of their busy day to snack on cheese cubes and crackers may be their biggest challenge.

Typical cubes: Morgan Freeman's character in the movie *Seven,* Tony Randall's character in *The Odd Couple,* and Jack Nicholson's character in *As Good As It Gets.*

If you're a cube-lover, you're most romantically compatible with others who also prefer cubes.

WHAT'S YOUR FOOD SIGN?

* **Free-spirited.** They are lively, colorful, and impulsive. While others may view their lifestyle as chaotic, stars and moons–lovers are comfortable in less-structured relationships.

* **Extroverts.** They are social butterflies and lean toward a dramatic flair. They enjoy being the life of the party.

* **Trendy dressers.** Their desire for the unusual makes stars and moons–lovers open to experimenting with new fashion trends. Their color choices tend toward the unusual.

* **Motivated.** Their personality traits make them creative contributors and motivators in the workplace as well as at home.

* **Partial to ethnic cuisines.** They enjoy spicy, exciting ethnic dishes, such as Thai, Mexican, and Indian.

* **Health-conscious.** Although they choose on-the-go lifestyles, most stars and moons–lovers recognize the importance of relaxation, exercise, and a healthy diet. They want to be fit so they are ready to take on the world.

But as a partner . . .

They like a romantic relationship, but they hesitate to settle down until they are absolutely certain they have found the right person. If you fall in love with a stars and moons–lover, be prepared to watch them thrive on testing the limits of their abilities. Since they're always looking for new experiences, such as traveling to exotic locations or taking up rock climbing or scuba diving, they will try to convince you to join them on their escapades.

Typical stars and moons characters: Chucky in *The Rugrats,* Marlin in *Finding Nemo,* and Rock Hudson's character in *Send Me No Flowers.*

If you're a stars and moons–lover, you'll be most romantically compatible with those who prefer cubes.

SLICE-LOVERS ARE:

* **Natural leaders.** They are driven and results-oriented. They expect 100 percent effort from themselves and those around them.

* **Competitive.** They gravitate toward everything that has an element of competition, and they will not tolerate defeat—that includes both work and romance!

* **Hard-working.** These are exciting individuals,

although they can appear to be so driven that they forget to enjoy the fruits of their labors. At work, others may say they're a bit hard to please, but slice-lovers will go above and beyond to reward others for a job well done.

* **Drawn to entertaining.** Slice-lovers enjoy family and friends and may make entertaining into a hobby, not unlike the prototype of a Martha Stewart homemaker. They not only don't complain about cooking the family's holiday meal, they volunteer for the job. They may set out to create a new recipe for a special occasion. For all their show, however, they are sensible eaters. Unless it's a special occasion, they like food to go, because they don't like to be interrupted when they are busy.

* **Conservative dressers.** They feel no need to stand out and draw attention to themselves, but they enjoy wearing high-quality, well-tailored clothing in striking colors. You might find them in red, black, and white and donning distinctive jewelry.

But as a partner . . .
Because they work so hard, you may not see as much of them as you like, and when you do, they may bring home co-workers for dinner or invite the neighbors over for a barbecue. Once they've assembled their group, they may suggest a competitive game of Trivial Pursuit, and those on their team better play to win. If you like everything at home in

working order, then these individuals may be a good match.

Typical slices: Martha Stewart, Leona Helmsley, and Angelica in *The Rugrats*.

Those who prefer slices are most romantically compatible with those who like shreds.

SHRED-LOVERS ARE:

* **Charismatic, energetic extroverts.** They thrive when they're the center of attention.

* **Concerned about looking good.** They believe in making a good first impression, so they devote a great deal of time and energy to their appearance, which includes keeping fit and trim as well as fashionable. They like bold colors and wear prominent jewelry.

* **Easily bored.** They are self-confident and are always seeking stimulation and novelty in all areas of their life, including food. Their need for excitement makes them dynamic team players at work and at home.

* **Love of the great outdoors.** Shred-lovers adore physical activities that get them outdoors.

But as a partner . . .

Because they are always on a search for a new challenge, they are fun to be with. They love the company of family and friends, so they may forever be organizing group events and outings. You may have to hold them back because these are the kind of people who suggest that all 24 relatives meet in Buenos Aries for Christmas. If you hook up with this personality type, you'll be biking and hiking and enjoying many outdoor picnics and barbecues.

Typical shreds: Bette Midler's character in *Ruthless People* and Catherine Zeta-Jones's character in *Intolerable Cruelty.*

Those who prefer shreds are most romantically compatible with cubes and slices or fellow shred personalities.

SUNBURST-LOVERS ARE:

* **Intellectual introverts.** They enjoy alone time as much as the company of others, and while they are devoted to friends and family, they may actively avoid loud gatherings.

* **Cautious in nature.** They are most happy when allowed to concentrate on their work or on one individual person.

* **Conservative in all things.** They avoid bold colors and risqué styles. They keep their clothing simple and choose jewelry that represents their individuality.

* **Insightful and intuitive.** They are excellent listeners and, when prompted, can always add interesting information to a conversation.

* **Solitude lovers.** Sunburst-lovers prefer hobbies that can be done on their own, such as exploring the world through books, magazines, and newspapers. They also regularly take time out for themselves and are much more prone to try to get a break in their day.

But as a partner . . .

Their introspective personalities and love of privacy may make dating a sunburst something of a challenge. However, they will become the devoted companions to those with whom they ultimately form relationships. You'll always know you're a "chosen" one.

Typical sunbursts: Robin Williams's character in *Awakenings* and Clint Eastwood's character in *Dirty Harry.*

Those who prefer sunbursts enjoy the freedom of the single life, but are open to relationships with like-minded individuals.

So, You're Out on a Date . . .

Cheese shapes are not something you'd be offered in a restaurant or even talk about at lunch. But our research on cheese shapes can give you important insight into a person's inner personality, so you don't want to miss the opportunity. All you have to do is lead the conversation in this direction.

. . . .

Example 1

Find something very unusual on the menu and point it out as a conversation-opener. Mention that the item reminds you of your nephew who likes critter-shaped candy, chocolate-rippled peanut butter, or some bizarre combination of foods.

Does your date:

> A) Laugh and say he/she wouldn't mind trying some?
> B) Look disgusted at the mere idea of "weird" food?

If the answer is "A," your date may think of food as fun and enjoyable, and may be willing to try new things. If the answer is "B," you may be lunching with a person who sees food as good food or bad food—a sign that he's on the rigid side.

The point is, a conversation like this can open up other

topics of conversation. At the mention of your niece or nephew, your lunch date might ask you if your family is close-knit or if you like kids. You can ask similar questions, and little by little, you're accumulating information.

. . . .

Example 2

You see your date pick out a few spicy pickles from the relish tray. From what you've learned so far, it is a tip-off that she's a pessimist. But you should not rush to judgment. It is still only a clue. Start a conversation that will give you an idea of her/his outlook on life.

Does your date:

A) Comment on the beautiful summer weather but follow it with a remark about having to "pay for it with a bad winter"?

B) Talk excitedly about an upcoming trip to Europe and comment on how lucky she was to get a great deal on the plane tickets, and how sure she is that the weather is going to be terrific?

In general, the spicy-pickle pessimist would come out with the first remark.

Example 3

You notice that your date heavily salts his food, so knowing what you've already read in this book, you might think you're dealing with a fatalistic personality. Or are you lunching with a guy whose sense of smell isn't particularly sharp? You need more information.

If your date doesn't use any salt, you may be with a health-conscious person, but one who may have underlying fears. Again, keep searching for more information.

• •

Have Some Matchmaking Fun

You can create an opportunity to observe others' food choices in your own home. Throw a party where you serve cheese in different shapes and a variety of other foods and drinks discussed in this chapter and the rest of the book. Then, watch what the guests choose. Since it's all in fun, you can use the personality profiles and match them with what's on your guests' plates. You may learn some interesting things about your friends, both married and single.

7

THE DINNER DATE:
ALWAYS
SOMETHING
SPECIAL

It can be formal or casual, just as long as you find an atmosphere where the conversation can get a little spicy.

• • • •

A few years ago, we considered studying the effect of garlic bread on the family dinner. The first question that arose was, "Do families actually eat dinner together?"

If you talk to busy couples, they might advise you to enjoy your dinner dates while you can. Once you settle down with family responsibilities, the TV trays come out and carryout comes in—life is too hectic and schedules too erratic for many families to enjoy sit-down dinners on a regular basis. Having a dinner date with your spouse may not become routine again until you becomes empty-nesters.

Be that as it may, the dinner date is a well-established tradition in our society. Dinner is also a great forum for "reading" your date as a potential partner. To illustrate how this works, try another quiz. As usual, select your preference from each of these 10 choices.

Which do you prefer?

1. A) Chicken and pea pods
   B) Szechuan chicken

2. A) Pot roast and carrots
   B) Ginger shrimp

3. A) Vegetable soup
   B) Minestrone soup

4. A) Tuna-noodle casserole
   B) Nachos with salsa

5. A) Broiled lamb chops
   B) Chili

6. A) Salmon with dill sauce
   B) Salmon teriyaki

7. A) Chicken salad
   B) Chicken curry

8. A) Cheese omelet
   B) Scrambled eggs with
      peppers and onions

9. A) Broiled pork chops
   B) Southern barbecue

10. A) Hamburger
    B) Beef taco

What your answers reveal about you:

* **If you chose "A" for at least seven out of the ten choices,** you are probably in a physically safe career, perhaps you work in an office or a bank. Maybe you are an accountant. You may prefer to garden or take long walks. If you like to sail, you may choose a heavy cruising boat and leave the "round the world" sailboat racing to the risk takers.

* **If you chose "B" for at least seven out of the ten choices,** you are likely to be in a high-risk career or tend to choose high-risk sports. Maybe you're a firefighter or police officer who likes to take whitewater rafting trips on the weekend. You could be an astronaut or a race-car driver (or at least desire to be one).

* **If your results were mixed**—most people fall in this category—you don't fit either description perfectly. You might work on a crew laying steel frames for skyscrapers, but you're a coin collector on the side. Maybe you're a banker who is saving your money to scale Mount Everest. Or, if you are a loner, you could be a banker planning a solo sail around the world.

How You Can Use This Information

This quiz was designed to provide insight into your tendency to choose a high-risk career or hobby, which is important to some people seeking a relationship. If, for instance, you are dating a computer programmer and you notice that he consistently orders spicy food, it wouldn't be surprising if you eventually learned that he works to support his passion for helicopter skiing or skydiving. This is how food choices can be used as signs to help you find out more about who you are dating.

Spicy or
Bland?

Noticing your date's preference for spicy food or bland food is a quick way to garner information about your date. The spicy or bland test came about some years ago as a result of a study we did on a group of firefighters who had lost their sense of smell. We wanted to find out if firefighters fit a particular personality profile, and we found that they fit society's general image of them. They are both risk-takers and altruistic. They enjoy living on the edge, at least to a degree, and the adrenaline rush associated with their profession is probably not unlike that experienced by soldiers, police officers, or emergency-room physicians.

> A preference for
> spicy or bland is
> a key food sign.

The divide between those who consistently prefer bland or spicy foods offers insight into personality. If you are dating a commodities trader who always asks for the extra-spicy Indian or Thai dishes or reaches for the hottest salsa, it is very likely that you are falling for a risk-taker. On the other hand, if your date is an accountant who swims for exercise and considers reading on the beach the perfect vacation but orders extra-hot garlic chicken, he may well be a risk-averse individual in disguise. Ask if he's always liked to eat hot food.

Watch the
Spices

Because of the variety of food available to us, it would be too confusing if you tried to match too many menu items to personality traits, so we devised a test to further define the bland versus spicy concept. After extensive testing on 800 people, we came up with specific "Spice Personalities."

Dinner is an ideal meal in which to do your own spice personality testing because many restaurant dishes are often associated by name or description with their herbs and spices. There is more than one spice listed for all our profiles, so even if you aren't familiar with one or two, you are bound to recognize some of the others. Observe your date's preferences over a few meals before drawing any of these conclusions.

• •

People who prefer:
Cayenne pepper, red crushed pepper, curry powder, chili powder, or mixed peppers are . . .

* **A bit rigid.** They like order at work and at home. You might think they are perfectionists, and they pay attention to detail—they even catch their own mistakes because they check their work. They may not delegate well, so it's possible they work long hours and don't like to waste their time on "frivolous" things.

141

* **Prone to take life seriously.** Maybe even too seriously. You can spot them in a dorm working on their papers weeks ahead of the deadline. They are enthusiastic, but not necessarily interested in a rich social life. They may confess that others tell them to lighten up because even hobbies can become more work than play.

* **Pack rats.** They like to keep everything in order, and they like things clean—but you may need to prod them to get rid of old papers and clothes. They may want to clean the house when you're in the mood for fun, which to them might be a waste of time.

* **Thrifty.** If you date these individuals, you may consider them stingy, but they are proud of it.

* **Logical thinkers.** They reason through decisions and don't like to talk in circles about a topic. And, if you get into a conflict, remember that they see life in black-and-white thinking.

. . . .

People who prefer:
Garlic, pepper, cloves, sage, and saffron are . . .

* **Lacking in self-confidence.** They might ask the wait staff about the best items on the menu and interrogate you about what you've ordered in the past.

These men and women may doubt their own ability to make independent choices and think for themselves. This may be a smokescreen of sorts, because these people are very competent and they may only lack confidence, or perhaps they ask these questions for their social value.

* **Easily intimidated.** These individuals might be unhappy if you invite them to be your date at a wedding or big company event, but they might readily accept an invitation to a small party or even a family barbecue. They prefer their own tight-knit family relationships.

* **Good at avoiding conflict.** They don't pick fights or join in gossip and criticism. They take no pleasure in alienating anyone.

. . . .

People who prefer:

Lemon peel, dill seed, sesame seed, oregano, and thyme are . . .

* **Worry warts.** They may seem serious over dinner because they tend to carry the weight of the world on their shoulders. They want everything to go well, but worry that it won't, and their concerns extend to work, family, health, and so forth.

* **Picky about punctuality.** They will mark the calendar for everything, even when it's time to have their tires rotated on their car—and yours, too.

* **Feeling the weight of the world on their shoulders.** They are concerned about everything that is happening in the world and feel you should be concerned, too. They believe this is normal—shouldn't we all worry about war, pollution, and the food served in the school-lunch program?

. . . .

People who prefer:
Parsley, chives, paprika, bay leaves, and sweet basil are . . .

* **Easy-going.** If the restaurant is closed when they walk up to the door, they're just as happy to cross the street and eat at another place. These individuals work hard, but they are too care-free to be perfectionist. But be prepared to double-check the tax return.

* **Headed for public life?** This personality type makes good politicians because of their pleasant demeanor and lack of negative traits. However, they might find drafting legislation a bit of a drag and may rely on others to amass knowledge of current affairs. The drawback to this is that they don't worry about their image and genuinely prefer to have a good time.

People who prefer:
Onion salt, celery seed, celery salt, garlic salt, and pick-ling spice are . . .

* **Outgoing.** These are the dramatic and theatrical types who like being the center of attention. These men and women are openly seductive and even sex-ually provocative—and they'll certainly kiss you in pub-lic. Lively and enthusiastic, they adore compliments.

* **Easily bored.** Since they seek new stimulation, you probably won't find them working behind a desk. They readily change jobs or occupations and hap-pily take on new projects, at least at first, before dis-satisfaction sets in. The men are aggressive athletes, and the women often have a very feminine style.

* **Sentimental.** They cry during movies. They are intu-itive, but tend to trust authority figures. Their relation-ships are strong, and romantic fantasies may break the boredom they find in routines.

. . . .

People who prefer:
Caraway seed, fennel, nutmeg, and anise seed are . . .

* **Charismatic.** They are often considered both brilliant and beautiful or handsome, and they enjoy power and success. They put in the effort to be the best and

enjoy the notion that they're unique and special—
they may also be drawn to you if they believe you're
superior, too.

* **Only want the best.** They look for the best doctor,
lawyer, beauty salon, and restaurant. This quest for
the best, however, can become annoying over time,
and they could appear snobbish and a bit patroniz-
ing as well.

* **Like to be treated special.** They like life at the top,
and they want to be treated like someone special.
Little annoyances of life bother them, and they
abhor waiting in lines. Being stuck in traffic with them
may be a deal-breaker in a relationship—you may
take it in stride, but they take it personally. They
expect ultimate respect for their talents and abilities.

* **Act on logic.** They may appear to lack empathy
because when they express themselves, they rely on
logic rather than emotions. These men and women
tend to be winners—and they believe in their own
ambitions and competence.

Chicken Is
Hot

Chicken is one of the most popular and versatile foods on the planet. From old-fashioned fried to marinated and grilled, chicken is enjoyed by just about everyone. It always has a place on the dinner table, and most families have favorite chicken recipes that are passed down from one generation to the next.

Many of us grew up with Kentucky Fried Chicken, which is why we used KFC as the basis of a study to find out what the spiciness of barbecue sauce says about personality and compatibility. We put 568 men and women through our usual personality tests, then asked them about their preference in condiments: blazing hot, sweet and spicy, and mild honey. Overall, 50 percent went for Blazing Buffalo, 32 percent went for Honey Barbeque, and 18 percent for Sweet and Spicy Candy Apple. This is what our results revealed:

THOSE WHO LIKE **BLAZING BUFFALO ARE. . .**

* **True blue.** They are loyal and true as friends and faithful in a relationship, though they tend to be possessive. They are more comfortable as followers than leaders. They prefer working in teams, and when a project goes well they happily give credit for the success to others.

* **Part of the team.** You'll likely find Blazing Buffalo lovers spending their leisure time engaged in noncompetitive sports or in team-oriented sports like bicycle racing, relay racing, or tug of war.

Blazing Buffalo people are most romantically compatible with other Blazing Buffalo lovers.

THOSE WHO LIKE **HONEY** BARBEQUE ARE. . .

* **Take-charge types.** These men and women are aggressive and achievement-oriented—in ancient times we might have called them the "conquerors." Today, they rise fast and become risk-taking entrepreneurs, CEOs, and leaders in many settings. And don't ask them to turn the other cheek. They respond to provocation in kind—and then some.

* **High rollers.** Honey Barbeque lovers enjoy the finer things in life and want to mingle with those they consider the "best." They like winners and they want to win, so they don't tolerate defeat well. Others might say they don't "suffer fools gladly."

Honey Barbeque sauce people are most romantically compatible with those who prefer Blazing Buffalo or Honey Barbeque.

WHAT'S YOUR FOOD SIGN?

* **Flamboyant.** Make these men and women the center of attention and they're happy. They are also unabashedly flirtatious and provocative risk-takers who enjoy new and exciting experiences in romance, work, and social situations. You may find these individuals in professions that land them in the public eye, such as actors, radio DJs, fashion designers, and others who thrive on public admiration.

Those who prefer Sweet and Spicy Candy Apple are most romantically compatible with those who prefer Blazing Buffalo.

How You Can Use This Information

You will probably see your date (and yourself) in more than one profile—this is natural because we tend to have a mixture of traits. However, in this study, certain personalities did emerge. For example,

Suggests a sushi bar . . . If this is his or her favorite food, you are likely dining out with a risk-taker, so get more information about their views on reckless risk or calculated risk.

Orders pasta . . . You may be dining with a dependent person, who tends to be a follower rather than a leader—and who could be a pessimist, too. Watch for the spices in the pasta dishes for more information.

Chooses pizza . . . Your date may be a bit of a worrier and could be a perfectionist. Watch how he or she handles bad service.

Asks for tacos . . . Look for other signs of a risk-taker—maybe it's a matter of degree.

Orders a cheeseburger . . . You're out with a traditional type of person, especially if they don't peruse the menu very long before ordering. Watch what else they order to get more insight.

Asks for a side french fries . . . Your date is probably a quiet, contemplative person who isn't impulsive.

Chooses meatloaf and mashed potatoes . . . Ordering these and other "comfort" foods means your date is not going to take many risks, but watch the dessert choice to learn more.

Dessert—The Problem with Chocolate

Dinner is the meal after which most people are likely to order dessert—especially if it is a special meal. Something special often leads to chocolate because it is so strongly associated with decadence. It is the ultimate "sinful dessert." Herein lies the problem when it comes to seeking food clues about your date. Why? Because virtually everyone likes chocolate.

We first ran into this dilemma when we investigated favorite flavors of Edy's/Dryers ice creams. Because virtually everyone likes it, we found we could not make correlations between personalities and flavor preferences for chocolate. Because it is practically universally enjoyed, we had to get into specific chocolate flavors before we could ascertain any similarities among personalities. This test demonstrates the concept of subdividing chocolate preferences. Choose one from each of the following:

Which do you prefer?

1. A) Milk chocolate
   B) Dark chocolate

2. A) Grapes
   B) Raisins

3. A) Apple pie
   B) Rhubarb pie

4. A) Plums
   B) Prunes

5. A) Malted milk balls
   B) Milk Duds

* **If you chose "A" four or more times,** you are an introverted, quiet, and contemplative person. People could say that you like to run or walk alone, or spend an afternoon exploring a bike trail by yourself. You enjoy nature and the outdoors. You may work alone, too; you could be a solitary computer consultant or a writer, and you might admit to spending hours on the Internet, but not in chat rooms. You can be found researching some favorite subject.

* **If you chose "B" four or more times,** you are an extrovert. You like large gatherings where your out-

going nature can shine. You may work in a fairly large office or in a retail business where you can be around other people most of the time. You prefer to work in teams, and you may play that way, too. Instead of hiking alone, you might join a club that takes adventure trips. You can be found in a bowling league or playing softball or volleyball.

* **We understand—you don't fit.** With this particular food-preference personality quiz, you may find mixed results. You can still use these food preferences to size up your date. You may find out that your date loves teamwork at the office, but prefers to spend his or her leisure time alone. It is not unusual to find that someone does not fit a pattern perfectly. As you probe, you may find that this person also loves going to a big party now and then.

Taking
the Cake

Consider the following first-date situations, which indicate your date's attitude toward chocolate desserts, and consider what they might mean about the other person.

Your date:

* **Orders a three-layer chocolate whipped cream torte—and makes no apology for it either.** Could it be that you are dining with a true hedonist, a person who enjoys food without guilt? Or, is this person just not very health-conscious?

* **Looks longingly at the dessert cart filled with chocolate desserts, but then refuses to order anything.** Could it be that you're out with a person who takes pride in self-discipline or self-denial? This person could also be a pessimist or someone who has trouble enjoying life. You could be having dinner with a person who won't reveal much.

* **Orders a chocolate dessert, but calls it "sinful" and uses some phrase like "just this once."** Is it possible your date could be a bit of Puritan? Actually, you might find that apologies for ordering chocolate may be the most common response in our society. We love our chocolate—for some, the richer the better—but we may find ourselves rationalizing and apologizing all over the place for it.

Those concerned about morals, even having too much fun, may cast a suspicious eye toward chocolate, which is why we might find desserts named "7 Layers of Sin" or "The Solid Chocolate Road to Hell." Of course, we also find chocolate Santas and Easter bunnies and Easter eggs, too.

Why Chocolate
Changes Mood

The chemical composition of chocolate is what gives it the ability to change how we feel. Not only does it have caffeine, it also contains a chemical known as theobromine, which is found in certain plants, including those from which we derive coffee and tea. Chocolate also contains tyramine and phenylethylamine, both of which tend to be arousing chemicals and have the ability to raise blood pressure. Chocolate is also high in magnesium, and it is possible that a craving for chocolate is actually a signal that the body is deficient in magnesium.

It's been shown that eating chocolate has the ability to reduce the sensation of pain in those who are already experiencing pain, which means that it acts as an analgesic agent. The way we perceive the taste of chocolate changes as we age, and a higher concentration of the taste is needed to gain the maximum amount of pleasure; hence, older individuals prefer a sweeter chocolate taste than younger people choose.

> Ask your date to share something chocolate and pay attention to the reaction.

When women head for chocolate during the days prior to the onset of menstruation, they may be self-medicating dysphoria, which is a state of mild sadness or unhappiness.

Dysphoria is not limited to women during their premenstrual days, however. It's possible that chocolate is a self-medication used by almost everyone, at least now and then, because sadness is a universal emotion. In addition, those who suffer from clinical depression also report an increase in chocolate cravings, which may be the body's unconscious effort to self-medicate.

A study conducted in England measured brain waves and found that the scent of chocolate was rated higher than either almond or strawberry in terms of the most pleasant smell. Chocolate certainly has a reputation as a "sexy" food (even though it didn't make it as a top turn-on scent in our sexual arousal tests). However, since it contains phenylethylamine, an amphetamine-like substance, it can produce a rush similar to what we feel when we fall in love. In fact, phenylethylamine is elevated during the early stages of infatuation and attraction. So, eating chocolate mimics the heady feeling we have early in our romances.

Chocolate
Stuff

Those who have a better sense of smell will enjoy chocolate more than those who have diminished ability to smell, because we need to detect the scent of chocolate in order to taste it. Hold your nose when you bite into even the most expensive piece of chocolate, and it will taste like chalk. In addition, the perception of chocolate changes as you keep eating it. Your first bites of a candy bar, for example, will taste better than your last. This phenomenon is part of a built-in satiety mechanism. If your perception didn't alter, you wouldn't stop eating. However, some people don't experience this with chocolate—I guess they could be called chocolate addicts. They tend to desire more and more chocolate, a phenomenon called moreishness.

Go Ahead,
Take a Bite

The answer to this one simple question can help you identify personality traits:

> If someone gave you a chocolate Easter egg, would you bite into it with the hope that it's *solid* or *hollow?*

Most people preferred hollow eggs, possibly because they got a quick burst of flavor or, put another way, they liked the fast route to a pleasant sensory experience. In terms of personality:

* **Those who preferred the hollow** bar like sudden thrills and adventure. You might find them at the climbing walls in athletic stores in preparation for their rock-

climbing vacation. In fact, it might not be a bad place to meet a potential mate if you're a bit of a thrill-seeker yourself. On the other hand, they may be on the impatient side, and could easily become dissatisfied with whatever is going on in their current lives.

* **Those who like the solid** chocolate better tend to be risk-aversive, or at least willing to move more slowly toward the pleasurable things in life. They tend to be satisfied with their current lives, although they may settle for less than they really want. These individuals would rather plan change so they can predict it. They may not be the most exciting people, but they are faithful and loyal.

So, You're Out on a Date . . .

Since dinner usually involves many choices, you can always open a conversation with

"What looks good to you?"

WHAT'S YOUR FOOD SIGN?

If the answer is:

* **"Not much"** . . . you may be in for a long evening. Conversations with pessimists tend to get old fast.

* **"Absolutely everything"** . . . the evening could get tiresome. The perpetual pollyanna for whom nothing goes wrong can be hard to deal with.

* **"Hmm, quite a few things"** . . . you're dealing with a genuine optimist—even an optimist will reject some choices.

The "what looks good to you?" question provides leads to fairly simple insights into personality. Another way to gather clues is to ask nonfood questions or make statements unrelated to food. And don't be afraid to be specific.

* "A friend of mine just went skydiving. Have you ever tried that?"

* "I'd rather go for a bike ride on Saturday than stay home and do chores. Wouldn't you?"

* "Everyone in my family is self-employed. That's my goal, too."

* "I just left my car at the shop, but it's okay. They do good work there."

* "I just saw (fill in name of recent sentimental or sad movie) with my sister—she really cried at the end. Have you seen it yet?"

* "There was a long wait for a table tonight."

The purpose of these comments is to match food choices with responses to statements. The following analysis is not meant to trick anyone, so I wouldn't want anyone to use it that way. But sometimes we say things we think others want to hear rather than revealing our true selves.

* If your date says he or she would never, ever, try sky-diving, then pay attention to the entrée ordered. If it's a plain burger or home-style pot roast, then you have two clues that you're dining out with a person for whom physical safety is important.

* If your date says, "I can't relax on Saturday until the laundry is done and the house is clean," and they ask for extra curry and peppers on their spicy chicken, it may be that your date is a serious, responsible person. That may be okay, as long as you don't feel as though you have to hide your frivolous nature!

* If your date says, "I could never work for myself—too risky," see if this person orders standard, not-too-spicy dinner fare. On the other hand, if he or she orders salty food, it's possible that they get bored easily and

look for new stimulation. They don't want to take on big responsibilities.

* If your date questions your judgment about your car mechanic and warns you to check your bill, they may order the garlic shrimp or ask if the pork loin dish is seasoned with sage. Actually, these individuals may not order a dish until the waiter says it's terrific.

* If your date laughs and talks about crying at movies, and then chooses food with fairly standard, sometimes sweet spices, it's possible you're getting the answer your date thinks you want. On the other hand, if your date can't stay away from the bowl of pickles, then you may be dining with a sentimental soul.

* If your date is in a foul mood because of the long wait, then he or she could be a driven personality, often quite successful. These individuals may look for the novel food items, such as the fennel salad. On the other hand, if he or she seems gloomy or feels bad about the wait, then see if he or she orders a plain burger or fish seasoned with lemon or dill. People who dislike lines can be individuals with a "special" complex and are prone to be driven and successful. They show their impatience with long lines with their glum behavior.

Home for
Dinner

The atmosphere at the dinner table speaks loudly about compatibility, and many a budding relationship has probably ended because the proverbial first dinner date ended badly. We all learn our dining skills at home around the dinner table—however often they may be. Though we have been ingrained with the vision of a happy family pleasantly chatting about the day's events, we know that this is mythology, at least in part.

> Dinner can tell you something about what your date's family life was like growing up.

As a psychiatrist, I've certainly listened to stories about family tensions that reveal themselves at the dinner table. It's become clear to me that many adults have a love-hate relationship with the whole idea of family dinners, usually based on past experiences. Eating together as a family has an enormous influence on the quality of family relationships. Every time a couple or family sits down together, they are creating a collective emotional climate, which may influence how they feel about the food served.

You may be able to gather impressions about a person's family life based on their demeanor over dinner. If your date seems nervous or doesn't talk, perhaps they grew up in a family where mealtimes were used as forums to criticize the kids. Or, if your date suggests having dinner where three big-screen TVs are on all the time, then perhaps this person doesn't view dinner as a chance to talk. Some people were raised to be silent while they eat, while others view dinner as the best place for conversation. You might as well learn this early in a relationship. If one person cherishes the dinner hour (at home or in a restaurant) as a meaningful time for closeness but the other person sees it as a chance to watch the news or read the newspaper, then compatibility could be an issue.

8

THE BAR SCENE:
WHAT VODKA
HAS TO SAY

It's the place to see and be seen, but get her personality prints on a glass of flavored vodka before you commit yourself.

• • • • •

Be it a cocktail lounge, nightclub, tavern, or bar, they all have one thing in common—they are the quintessential gathering places for singles to meet other singles. In every town across America (and in lots of other countries, too), there is at least one place where women (usually in pairs or groups) and men (often alone) gather (usually on a Friday night) to see and be seen in the hope that, just maybe, a drink (or two) will lead to romance.

Alcohol in all its forms has the reputation of lubricating social interaction by lowering inhibitions and helping people to relax, though it can also interfere with socializing if people drink too much.

Why We
Drink
Alcohol

For the most part, appropriate times and places to consume alcohol are related to cultural norms. You may consider drinking wine or beer with lunch odd, perhaps even suspect, but feel it is quite acceptable to go to happy hour most nights after work.

For many people, alcohol has a link to larger moral issues, which is why most of us have some set of rules that guide the times, places, and amounts we consider acceptable. Almost every substance that is mind-altering to one degree or another has supporters and detractors, which is another reason that customs develop around its use.

> People don't go to bars because they enjoy the taste of alcohol any more than they drink coffee because it tastes so good.

We do know that people don't go to bars just because they enjoy the taste of alcohol any more than they drink coffee because it tastes good. We also don't consume alcohol just to self-medicate and change our mood. If that were the case, people would stick with drinks that delivered the most alcohol, such as 150-proof spirits that deliver alcohol to the brain quickly. But we don't do that, because alcohol is related to events and the atmosphere we create for drinking.

Put another way, spending the evening in a wine bar wouldn't be much fun if patrons guzzled entire bottles of wine within 30 minutes and then passed out. No, that would violate the social norms, which call for alcohol to be part of a bigger experience that could include anything from watching a ball game to playing pool to meeting a new romance.

For our purposes here, we aren't looking to analyze the reasons people drink or go to bars to meet the opposite sex. Rather, we are looking to find out what a person's preferred drink says about his or her personality. We did not plan our study to find out the personality differences between beer-drinkers and wine-drinkers, or those who prefer bourbon over gin. This is a case where the phrase "all things being equal" applies, because we focused our research on the variations of one type of alcohol: vodka.

The popularity of vodka and the trend toward a variety of flavors made it an easy choice. It was also an economic equalizer because flavored vodkas are priced identically within a brand. With all external influences being equal, internal factors must be the primary motivating force for choosing one flavor instead of another.

As with all other food choices we have examined in this book, keep in mind that individuals are influenced by a multitude of both conscious and unconscious processes, from perceptions of both alcohol in general to vodka in particular, both past and present. The issue of our comfort with the familiar operates as well. In terms of alcohol, plain vodka is safe, in the same way that cheese slices (as opposed to cheese shaped like stars and moons) are safe. Vanilla vodka may strike some as being just as odd as vodka-flavored ice cream.

> Sipping a flavored vodka is a sign that you're willing to take a risk.

Other influences include the relative pleasure one finds in the vodka flavor. Those who dislike vodka altogether (or perhaps disapprove of alcohol) may choose the strongest flavor because they want to mask the alcohol taste. Those

who like the inherent vodka flavor would likely shift towards the weakest flavor, which would allow the natural aroma or flavor to dominate. The same kind of associations may exist with the flavors we tested as well.

Some differences between men and women may also influence flavor choice. For example, women have a better ability than men to sense the taste of bitter, and the super-tasters of both sexes have more taste buds and far greater taste ability than a normal taster.

Regardless of these individual influences, our personality fingerprints are imprinted in every choice we make, including vodka preferences. So, just as we eat what we are, we also drink what we are.

A special note: Some individuals develop or are predisposed to alcoholism, a disease with its own profiles and risk factors. Though a serious and important issue, it is outside the scope of this book. Let me just say clearly that the information in this chapter addresses individuals who do not have problems with alcohol and consume it only in moderate amounts.

What's Your
Vodka Sign?

By now, you're familiar with our research methods, including the many hours of personality tests we conduct to validate our findings. For this project we recruited 567 adults who had to choose among peach, vanilla, cranberry, citrus, raspberry, and orange vodkas. We also correlated the results of partners in a relationship to help us determine long-term compatibility.

Vanilla and raspberry were tied at 22 percent as the most popular flavor in our test group. Orange and citrus tied for second at 18 percent, followed by cranberry (15 percent), and peach (5 percent).

VANILLA VODKA-
LOVERS . . .

* **Crave the company of others.** These are impulsive and emotionally driven individuals who are most comfortable among other people. They're hardworking and crave acceptance, and they do well, either at work or school, with a structured environment.

They'll do almost anything to be desired by others, even to their own detriment.

* **Are hard on relationships.** These men and women develop intense romantic relationships quickly, but fall out of love just as fast. They often hold a grudge, too. Because of their impulsive nature, vanilla vodka–lovers should be careful to avoid excessive gambling, compulsive shopping, reckless driving, and unsafe sex.

Typical vanillas: Glenn Close's character in *Fatal Attraction.*

Those who prefer vanilla vodka are most romantically compatible with others who prefer vanilla vodka and are least compatible with those who prefer peach or raspberry.

RASPBERRY VODKA– LOVERS . . .

* **Feel self-important.** These individuals are driven, success-oriented, self-confident, and natural leaders. They are charming people and expect the very best from themselves and from everyone else as well. They do not tolerate defeat.

* **Are impatient.** These men and women do not easily suffer fools, are impatient, and are easily annoyed by the day-to-day ups and downs in life, including wait-

ing in lines. They tend to be aggressive drivers, often getting furious if stuck in rush-hour traffic.

Typical raspberries: The public personas of Donald Trump and Martha Stewart, and Michael Douglas's character in *Wall Street.*

Raspberry vodka–lovers are most romantically compatible with other raspberry vodka–lovers and are least compatible with those who prefer vanilla vodka.

ORANGE VODKA–
LOVERS . . .

* **Have wonderful virtues.** Kind adjectives define these men and women. They are empathic, understanding, easy-going, well-adjusted, dependable—you name it. They also make the perfect spouse or parent.

Typical oranges: The public personas of Katie Couric and Tom Hanks.

Orange vodka–lovers are most compatible with those who prefer citrus-flavored vodka and are least compatible with peach vodka–lovers and raspberry vodka–lovers.

* **Are nonconforming.** These individuals are sympathetic with the anti-establishment crowd. They also tend to be pessimistic doom-sayers and are frequently viewed by others as irritable and cranky.

Typical citruses: The public personas of Larry David and the ogre Shrek.

Citrus vodka–lovers are most compatible with other citrus vodka–lovers and are least compatible with those who prefer cranberry vodka.

* **Romantics.** These are workaholics, aggressively initiating projects at work or at home, to the point where they have no downtime. They're not showy individuals and prefer to live in a modest manner. They do best when they are totally in control of the situation, whether at home, at work, or in romantic relationships.

Typical cranberries: The public persona of Brad Pitt and Courteney Cox's character, Monica, in *Friends.*

Those who like cranberry vodka are the universal romantics and therefore are romantically compatible with everyone!

* **Lots of fun to be around.** These men and women are lively, dramatic, and enthusiastic—the proverbial life of the party. They crave novelty in work, social relationships, and sexual encounters.

* **In need of instant gratification.** They want immediate satisfaction in all aspects of their lives. They live for now, not for the future. Their sexually provocative, flirtatious, and seductive behavior, combined with their overly trusting nature, may lead to a series of intimate but superficial relationships for which they later feel regret.

Typical peaches: Diane Keaton's character in *Looking for Mr. Goodbar,* the character of Jerry Seinfield, the Donkey in *Shrek,* Kim Cattrall's character, Samantha, in *Sex and the City,* and Debra Messing's character in *Will and Grace.*

Peach vodka–lovers are most romantically compatible for a long-term relationship with those who prefer citrus vodka and are relatively incompatible with those who prefer any other vodka flavor.

Throw a
Party

Since bars offer far more spirits than vodka, the best way to get a real read on someone you are interested in is to throw a party. Offer specialized drinks using flavored vodkas. Make it a worthwhile food-signs adventure by serving cheese in the variety of shapes as discussed in Chapter 6 and the snacks you will be reading about in Chapter 10. Serve the vodka drinks chilled and then make a game of talking about the flavors people choose. Of course, this should only be done in a good-natured, playful way, but . . .

* **Match up your guests who choose vanilla and see if they fit the description.** Do they fall in and out of love quickly, and are they extroverts? Ask them why they chose the vanilla-flavored drink.

* **Are the raspberry vodka–lovers really leaders?** Did they volunteer to lead your game, or are they griping about something that irritated them earlier in the day? You might find them already socializing because they tend to like each other best.

* **Will the orange vodka–drinkers join the game without an argument?** Don't be surprised to find out that they are the old reliables who showed up at the party on time.

* **Find out if the orange vodka–lovers gravitate toward those who like citrus.** These potential curmudgeons may gravitate toward each other to talk about their plans to change the world. If there is a peace rally in town, you can expect the citrus-lovers to show up late!

* **Those who choose cranberry-flavored vodka may be the last to show up.** After all, work keeps them so busy, they wonder why everyone else isn't so dedicated. You might find them working the crowd because they are hopeless romantics and want to get along with everyone.

* **Are some of your guests entertaining everyone else with dramatic the-date-from-hell stories?** Chances are, you'll find them with a peach vodka drink in their hand. Watch them compete with each other for the best story and have the rest of your guests take a vote.

Watching
Your Dates

The problem with vodka, like coffee, is that not everyone likes it, so you won't be able to pick up the food clues that they can provide. But there is an ideal setting for a date that hardly anyone ever thinks of going to anymore. Too bad, because it's a place a date is sure to love—and where you can read some interesting food signs. It's the ice cream parlor.

9

THE ICE CREAM PARLOR: **A LITTLE OLD-FASHIONED ROMANCE**

Your date's favorite **flavor** could be the food sign that will melt your heart.

•••••

Just like our sexual arousal studies, our ice cream studies were attention-grabbers. I've been interviewed hundreds of times on serious subjects related to my research, but after the ice cream studies, the topic always turned to ice cream. Just like everyone else, reporters couldn't get enough of it.

It wasn't all that long ago—before household freezers and mass production—that ice cream was served only on special occasions. There is still something about ice cream that makes it special. If a survey were performed today, however, we would find at least one flavor, if not two or three, in the freezer of most typical households. If there are older folks in the household, there might even be a carton of the once-very-popular Neapolitan—the old standards vanilla, chocolate, and strawberry together in one carton. Ice cream is a 10.8 billion dollar industry in the United States, which probably proves that the label "America's favorite dessert" is accurate.

Everyone Likes
Ice Cream

Among children and even many grown-ups, ice cream is considered a treat or a reward. It's always linked with a happy occasion—birthday parties, carnivals, a day at the beach. You will rarely, if ever, find ice cream served at gatherings of family and friends after a funeral—no matter how sweltering the weather.

Ice cream is an ideal food sign. It is one of the few universally enjoyed foods, so it eliminates the fear of trying something new. It is consumed widely among all races and ethnic groups, religions, economic groups, and others we might label as belonging to "subcultures." In other words, you can find rap singers, artists, accountants, and even ministers wandering a street fair licking an ice cream cone.

An Emotional
Investment

It might seem ridiculous that anyone would care *deeply* about a food and all its variations, but we do. Unlike brussels sprouts or baked beans or chipped beef, ice cream has a whimsical quality and, indeed, carries emotional value. Despite its availability, it remains, on an emotional level, a little on the "sinful" side. No one ever thinks of baked beans as a luxury item that we only get if we're "good."

Ice cream's association with a treat or reward imbues it with a strong, almost magical aura, so few people pay much attention to its nutritional value. The emotional investment in it is so high that it

Cone or Dish

· ·

We found it kind of interesting that everyone we surveyed denied ever eating ice cream directly from a carton. Everyone said that at home they scoop their ice cream into a dish, but we think it's more likely that our participants had reservations about actually admitting they ate ice cream from a carton.

Through our studies, we found a few other interesting facts about ice cream "customs":

* Regardless of flavor preference, everyone preferred sugar cones over plain cones.

* All ice cream personalities preferred eating ice cream in a cone—except chocolate chip-lovers. They were the only ones who preferred ice cream in a cup.

* Vanilla or chocolate chip–lovers preferred single to double scoops.

* Strawberries-and-cream or butter pecan–lovers preferred double over single scoops.

* Double chocolate chunk or banana cream pie–lovers were equally divided between single and double scoop preferences.

WHAT'S YOUR FOOD SIGN?

is indulged in despite the perception that it's loaded with fat, calories, and sugar. Some of us work around this killjoy factor by opting for some combination of low-fat, no-fat, no-sugar-added, or soy- or rice-based variety. We even choose double fudge chocolate frozen yogurt or sorbet and convince ourselves that it's health food.

Your ice cream flavor preference remains the same from childhood through your adult life.

It would be easy to say that marketing alone has created our emotional attachment to ice cream, but that would be missing the point that the great majority of us acquired a taste for it in childhood. In fact, we delineate our flavor preference in ice cream approximately the same time personality traits tend to become fixed—around age 7. And like personality, ice cream preferences tend to be stable throughout adult life. Unlike our choice among political candidates, when it comes to our favorite ice cream flavor, the vast majority of people are not "undecided."

The Ultimate
Nostalgia

Ice cream is sweet and fat-laden (even if fat substitutes only make it seem that way), and so is breast milk, which is one reason why ice cream is associated with comfort. Even on television and in movies, someone who has been dumped or left or longs for love (usually women, but not always) can be seen eating ice cream straight from the container. When a character is sad, a friend might offer ice cream—usually something with chocolate in it—to brighten their spirits.

Unconscious memories of breast milk or its substitutes essentially cause these associations. And, beyond that, the act of eating the ice cream is different than that of eating all other foods—both sexes, regardless of age are allowed to lick an ice cream cone! We consider it one of our parental duties to pass the art of licking a cone on to the next generation. Looking at this psychoanalytically, the way we eat ice cream conjures up long-forgotten memories of suckling at the nipple.

> Your favorite ice cream flavor provides clues about who you are as an individual.

For all these reasons, ice cream is a good food to study—and a good food with which to search for someone's true essence. As you will see, our favorite flavors provide clues about who we are as individuals. You may learn quite a bit about your companion if you suggest going out for ice cream.

You and your date are at the ice cream parlor and you must choose your favorite flavor. Which one of these 10 would you pick?

1. Vanilla

2. Double chocolate chunk

3. Strawberries and cream

4. Banana cream pie

5. Chocolate chip

6. Butter pecan

7. Strawberry

8. Coffee

9. Mint chocolate chip

10. Rocky road

What's Your
Ice Cream Sign?

We did several studies that involved hundreds of men and women, single and married, ranging in age from 20 to 69. We also gave these people detailed personality tests so we could correlate their flavor preferences with personality traits.

* **Dependent and needy.** You are colorful, at times impulsive, and easily suggestible. An idealist, you don't mind taking risks, and you see your hectic schedule as a means to achieving the high goals you have set for yourself. You are a private person who enjoys close relationships with others.

As a date:
You are most comfortable in a close and secure relationship.

Typical vanillas: A "lovelorn" housewife who enjoys soap operas and romantic novels.

Those who choose vanilla will likely be most romantically compatible with a partner who favors rocky road. Vanilla-lovers are also romantically compatible with others who love vanilla, too.

* **Self-absorbed.** You like being the center of attention and tend to be somewhat dramatic. Other adjectives to describe you include lively, charming, flirtatious, and seductive. You tend to like novelty, and you get bored easily, especially by routine. You enjoy clothing, and people consider you well-dressed, which goes along with your creative nature.

* **Gullible.** Enthusiastic and an extrovert, you are also sensitive and easily suggestible. Other people can influence you easily because you may trust them too much, which is why you're a follower rather than a leader. As an intuitive person, you tend to play hunches rather than rely on logic.

As a date:

You thrive on intimate, close relationships and can quickly become absorbed in romantic fantasy.

Typical double chocolate chunks: An actor or actress—a very feminine woman or a macho man.

Those who prefer double chocolate chunk will be most compatible with a partner whose favorite ice cream is either butter pecan or chocolate chip.

* **The nervous type.** An introvert, you do not handle the stresses of life well. In fact, at times they may overwhelm you and make you feel inadequate. Others can make you feel guilty, and you easily become irritable and cranky.

As a date:
Your low self-esteem and vision of seeing the glass as half-empty will give you trouble in finding a long-term relationship.

Typical strawberries and creams: The public persona of the curmudgeon TV journalist Andy Rooney—in fact, journalists and columnists in general, along with bureaucrats and receptionists in the complaint and return departments of retail stores.

Strawberries and cream–lovers are most likely to have a partner whose favorite flavor is chocolate chip.

* **An old softy.** Well-adjusted, easy-going, and empathetic are just a few adjectives to describe your good and friendly nature.

As a date:
You'd make the perfect spouse and parent because you are already the perfect child.

Typical banana cream pies: Bill Cosby and Phylicia Rashad's characters on *The Cosby Show.*

Those who prefer banana cream pie are likely be most romantically compatible with a partner whose favorite ice cream is vanilla, double chocolate chunk, strawberries and cream, banana cream pie, chocolate chip, or butter pecan.

* **Most likely to succeed.** You are ambitious, with a competitive streak that leads others to call you a go-getter. You like to be on top and conquer whatever you go after. Some would call you a visionary.

As a date:
Though you are always charming in social situations, you may find yourself butting heads with someone of your same style, especially because you enjoy being catered to.

Typical chocolate chips: Leaders of industry, like Donald Trump and Martha Stewart, and graduates voted the most likely to succeed.

Chocolate chip–lovers are most romantically compatible with those who choose either butter pecan or double chocolate chunk.

IF YOU LIKE BUTTER PECAN, YOU ARE . . .

* **Principled above all else.** You don't break the rules, and because of your scruples, you set high standards for yourself and everyone else. People would describe you as intelligent, conscientious, moral, and a perfectionist. You love to work, and you're a perfect worker—never wasting time or procrastinating. You're a take-charge person who loves to work and pay attention to the most trivial details. When you play a game or a sport, you show an aggressive, competitive side, although you're quick to criticize your own performance.

As a date:

You are sexually reserved and you may have difficulty expressing your true feelings to someone for fear of hurting his or her feelings.

Typical butter pecans: Marcia Cross's character in *Desperate Housewives,* and the public persona of George Hamilton.

Butter pecan–lovers are most romantically compatible with those who prefer mint chocolate chip.

IF YOU LIKE STRAWBERRY, YOU ARE . . .

* **Content to live in another's shadow.** You tend to be a follower rather than a leader and are happy working behind the scenes and out of the limelight. If the project succeeds, you enjoy the rewards of group success. You are successful as part of a team, and you have no desire or need to be elected captain, hired as the CEO, or promoted to boss.

As a date:

You don't fall head-over-heels in love at first sight, but once you commit to a relationship, which is usually after you get to know someone very well, you remain loyal and supportive. As a spouse, you will also make a good best friend.

Typical strawberries: Vice President Dick Cheney and perhaps his wife, Lynne.

Strawberries are most romantically compatible with those who prefer strawberry, rocky road, mint chocolate chip, and vanilla.

IF YOU LIKE COFFEE, YOU ARE . . .

* **Living for the moment.** Lively, dramatic, seductive, and flirtatious are the words that describe your personality. You think life is great and people might say you live it with gusto. You don't think too much about the future but would rather embrace the passion of the moment. You throw yourself headfirst into everything, so you sometimes find yourself overcommitted. You think nothing of starting something new and leaving other things half-done.

As a date:
People of the opposite sex find you appealing but same-sex acquaintances may consider you a threat. You're easily bored by the same old things, so you need a partner who can be stimulating company.

Typical coffees: The public persona of Paris Hilton.

Coffee ice cream–lovers are most romantically compatible with those who prefer strawberry.

* **A cynic.** Your ambition and confident skepticism mean that you would make a good lawyer. You enjoy being argumentative and aren't fully satisfied until you get under the other person's skin. This makes you a contrary sort, which might help you in business.

As a date:
You have a personality that can wreak havoc upon your romantic relationships. Your belief that "good things don't last" means you are frugal and cautious about planning the future. If you use this trait wisely and tame it down a bit, you can succeed at achieving a happy and successful relationship.

Typical mint chocolate chips: James Spader's character on *Boston Legal*.

Mint chocolate chips are most romantically compatible with others who also choose mint chocolate chip as their favorite.

* **Experienced at getting what you want.** You are charming and engaging in social situations, but you are aggressive and goal-directed at the office. You may even own the business. In your drive to succeed, you could sometimes inadvertently hurt other people's feelings.

* **Comfortable with all the trimmings of success and aren't self-conscious about it.** You tend to be on the cynical side and are known to lose your temper when faced with life's inconveniences, and are particularly impatient when forced to wait in line.

As a date:
Despite your success, you are sensitive and a good listener. You don't like criticism, but you may come around if your lover adopts a cajoling attitude.

Typical rocky roads: President George Bush and his 2002 opponent, Senator John Kerry.

Rocky roads will do best romantically with others who also choose rocky road.

Degrees of
Vanilla

When we began to study vanilla and its variations, I was reminded of the 1960s movie *The Graduate,* in which a supposedly wise man tells Dustin Hoffman's character that the future could be read in one word: "plastics." Forty years later, I would change that single word to "vanilla."

Many converging trends support this prediction, including the dynamic fluctuation in the U.S. population. The fastest-growing population segment is Hispanic, with Mexican immigrants making up the majority. Vanilla is an immensely popular flavor in Mexico, which means it will become prominent in the United States, since waves of immigration influence domestic trends in food, as well as in clothing or movies or vacation spots.

Another reason that vanilla will top other flavors is in the way trends occur. A half-century ago, we preferred simple flavors. Today we have more complex flavors. The shift has gone from bitter to sweet and fatter—just like the new trends in coffee discussed in Chapter 5. In addition, the U.S population is aging, and with aging comes a diminished ability to smell. Since the sense of smell is most important for flavor perception, we will see greater attempts to enhance otherwise bland tastes, which is one reason the intense smell of vanilla will be added to more foods.

Even though vanilla is an intense and powerful flavor and scent, vanilla is culturally defined as meaning bland and unexciting. It also happens to be one of the most frequently reported smells that induce nostalgia for childhood. So, at a time when much of our society is apprehensive and uncertain, it isn't surprising that we'd unconsciously use the "smell and taste" of safety. It's as if we believe we can re-create a time in the past when we felt safe.

So, for myriad reasons, the United States is moving toward "vanillatization," and we can see it clearly in ice cream consumption. Right now, vanilla accounts for more than 20 percent of ice cream sales, and 40 percent of households—32 million—buy vanilla ice cream at least once a year.

Because it's so popular, it was logical to study vanilla ice cream separately, so we enlisted 630 men and women and put them through personality assessments, matching those to preferences among four different kinds of vanilla ice cream.

Vanilla bean turned out to be the favorite among the vanillas at 50 percent. This was followed by vanilla (39 percent), French vanilla (8 percent), and double vanilla (3 percent). We also then correlated the results with married spouses in order to determine compatibility of preference—just as we did with other ice cream flavors.

WHAT'S YOUR FOOD SIGN?

* **Sincere and easy-going.** They are agreeable and well-adjusted. They seem like the ideal partner (or friend or parent) because they're patient, under-standing, and empathetic. These individuals are serious and mean it when they say they care about other people's feelings, even above their own. They make ideal teachers and psychiatrists, and are great as coworkers or supervisors. In any capacity, they are a pleasure to be around.

As a date . . .
Those who prefer double vanilla are the universal romantics.

Typical double vanillas: Noah Wyle's character in *ER*.

Double vanillas are romantically compatible with everyone. Too bad there are so few of them!

* **Dapper and debonair.** There is nothing "vanilla" about these men and women. Natural actors, they enjoy being the center of attention, and they react to the slightest challenge with a dramatic flair and exaggerated emotion.

As a date . . .

They are seductive and sensually provocative and crave novelty in all their pursuits—at work, at play, and at home.

Typical vanillas: Jessica Rabbit in *Who Killed Roger Rabbit?*

Those who prefer vanilla ice cream are most compatible with others who also prefer vanilla.

VANILLA BEAN–
LOVERS ARE . . .

* **Not good at putting their lives in balance.** They are detail-oriented and conscientious to a fault, which makes them perfect employees but they struggle trying to keep their work and personal lives in balance. They have strong opinions about how things should be done. They also have a clear sense of right and wrong.

As a date . . .

They like to take charge, but your love life could suffer as a result of the lopsided balance in their lives.

Typical vanilla beans: Tony Randall's character in *The Odd Couple.*

Vanilla bean–lovers are most romantically compatible with those who prefer either vanilla or vanilla bean ice cream.

* **The homebody type.** They function best in familiar, safe, secure relationships. They make loving and supportive spouses, and don't crave novelty in either romantic or social relationships. They tend to follow more than lead, so they will avoid the spotlight and work best in group settings.

As a date . . .

Typical French vanillas: Tom Hanks's character in *Forrest Gump* and Talia Shire's character in *Rocky*.

Those who prefer French vanilla are most romantically compatible with others who also prefer French vanilla.

So, You're Out
on a Date . . .

When men and women want my advice about finding true love, I usually tell them to forget about bars and Internet chat rooms or dating services. Hang out wherever ice cream is sold!

Consider the chances of meeting someone at a bar versus a place that serves ice cream. For such a universally loved food item, why don't we see more singles nights or "Happy Hour Specials" at the ice cream stand? Perhaps this will be the beginning of a new matchmaking trend. What better way to gain insight into your new love's personality (and your own) than picking out your flavors and hanging out for a while at the ice cream parlor or the frozen dessert section of the supermarket?

If you decide to sign up with an online matchmaking service, you can still find out about a potential date's personality traits. When you're first getting to know someone, suggest a list of favorites—favorite band, movies, vacation spot—and don't forget to ask: "What's your favorite ice cream flavor?"

10

PASS THE PRETZELS—
OR MAYBE THE CHIPS

A date to a ballgame or the movies **can** reveal a lot about who you are with— even if there isn't much conversation going on.

• • • • •

Three square meals a day . . .

If Americans were taking this nutritional advice seriously, our supermarkets would look a lot different. Snack food aisles have proliferated into a multi-billion-dollar industry. It is estimated that the average person eats about 22 pounds of snacks—plus 3.5 pounds of chocolate—a year.

We've elevated snack food to a "cuisine" of its own. Events like movies and sporting events just wouldn't seem right if we couldn't munch while watching. Even health clubs have snack bars! This gives us license to eat day and night and makes it quite convenient for a little food sign research.

What's Your
Snack Sign?

Like our taste in clothing, our taste in snack food is part of our individuality. Just as it is with personality, our preference for the same snack food remains relatively stable for life. Consumers tend to remain loyal to the same type of snack, though not always to the same brand or flavor. When potato chip–lovers have a taste for something different, they may venture toward a barbecued or vinegar-flavored chip, but probably not toward a tortilla chip.

As with clothing, our preference for a certain snack food expresses our individuality.

For the sake of argument, any food could be considered a snack if not eaten as part of a meal, and any snack food could be part of a meal—like chips with a sandwich. For the purpose of our study, however, we kept with tradition. Our 800 volunteers went through all the necessary detailed personality tests in order for us to come up with our individual snack food profiles. Once again, you have the chance to pick *your* favorite:

A) Potato chips
B) Tortilla chips
C) Pretzels
D) Snack crackers
E) Cheese curls
F) Meat snacks
G) Nuts
H) Popcorn

PEOPLE WHO PREFER
POTATO CHIPS ARE . . .

* **High achievers.** Ambitious and successful, these men and women enjoy the trappings of the good life they've gone after and earned. They disdain life's inconveniences, and they're vocal about it, too. Many people find this a less than attractive trait,

especially if they are with a chip-lover when they are stuck in traffic or delayed at the airport.

* **Fair warning:** These are competitive individuals in all areas of life, and they always come prepared, whether it's for a game of "friendly" tennis or Trivial Pursuit or for negotiating the best price for a house or choosing stocks for their portfolio.

As a date . . .
They are as exuberant about family life as they are about their personal ambition. They enjoy the successes of their mates and children, too, because they want to be surrounded by those who also want and seek the best.

Potato chip–lovers are most compatible with others who like potato chips or pretzels.

PEOPLE WHO PREFER TORTILLA CHIPS ARE . . .

* **The best that they can be.** This is the kind of person you'd want to be with if you were marooned on an island. They are perfectionists through and through— they'll go back and redo something over again if it means going from an "A" to an "A+."

* **On the side of the little guy.** Their concerns extend beyond their own actions to society, and they don't like inequity and injustice. Because they are con-

cerned with how others feel, they make good house-guests and, if you date them, they are always on time. They are also personally conservative.

As a date . . .

If you want a proper partner who will always behave and make you look good at office functions, take a tortilla chip–lover. Because they are concerned individuals, they will always be responsible about money and family budgets, will keep the house orderly, and make sure that everyone in their family has doctor and dentist appointments and takes their vitamins.

When it comes to compatibility, tortilla chip–lovers should stick with each other.

PEOPLE WHO PREFER PRETZELS ARE . . .

* **Quirky, but fun.** Pretzel people do not like routine, and they're always in search of something novel and new. Lively and energetic, they thrive in the world of abstracts because the day-to-day world is so mundane. They overcommit because they don't plan their time well, which is also why they will always have projects in various states of completion.

* **Fad followers.** Pretzel-lovers like to wear comfortable but attractive clothes, and they tend to follow fads in many things. You may find them with an

attic filled with Beanie Babies or an old beer can collection.

As a date . . .

If a pretzel-lover is your partner, you'll always have fun because they enjoy life and other people want to be around them, too. This could be a drawback if you are the jealous type because they do like to flirt. However, pretzel-lovers have trust in a partner—possibly too much—because they tend to rely on intuition and emotion more than on logic to make decisions.

Pretzel-lovers get along well with other pretzel people but they may find happiness with those who prefer potato chips or cheese curls.

PEOPLE WHO PREFER
SNACK CRACKERS ARE . . .

* **Shy and introspective.** These individuals make their decisions based on logic, and they may think about them for a long time, too. They may not talk about their choices because they don't want to debate. They are well-rounded and have a multitude of interests, which means a variety of projects compete for their time and attention.

* **Seekers of solitude.** They are most creative when they can be by themselves and forget about their responsibilities. They do not like interruptions.

As a date . . .

Snack cracker-lovers are willing to please. They hate confrontation and will avoid a fight for the simple reason that they don't want to hurt anyone's feelings. These individuals may be the most likely candidates for Internet romances.

People who prefer snack crackers should look for a partner who prefers pretzels.

*****Down-to-earth.** These are the moralists among us, and they practice what they preach, in that they are always proper, conscientious, and principled. Their sense of right and wrong guides their behavior, and they treat everyone else in the same fair way. Status doesn't mean much to them. The most succinct word to describe them would be "integrity." Some might consider the downside of the cheese curl-personality to be that everything around them must be as neat as a pin. They detest a cluttered desk, and they attend to every detail at work and at home.

As a date . . .

If you partner with a cheese curl-lover, you will be with a planner who is prepared for any eventuality. So, you'll always have spare batteries for the flashlights and first-aid supplies at the ready. When in the home of a cheese curl-lover, you'll feel like you can eat off the kitchen floor.

Cheese curl–lovers are most compatible with people who prefer potato chips or tortilla chips.

* **Surrounded with friends.** These are gregarious men and women who enjoy being among others. They make true and loyal friends and are known for their generosity. Some might say they are generous to a fault because they will make extraordinary self-sacrifices to please others.

As a date . . .
Their overtrusting nature can lead to emotional turmoil, especially when breaking up with a lover. They have a tendency to jump into rebound relationships.

Meat snack–lovers should stick together, but they can be compatible with potato chip–lovers.

* **Dependable.** These are easy-going, level-headed individuals who usually go with the flow. You can always rely on them, especially during an emer-

gency. They stay calm while others panic, and they like change.

As a date . . .
They are likely to show up on time for your date and won't mind if you decided to modify the plan for the evening.

Those who like nuts tend to be most compatible with other nut-lovers.

PEOPLE WHO PREFER
POPCORN ARE . . .

* **Achievement-oriented.** Like potato chip–lovers, these individuals tend to be very successful in life, only they are extremely modest and humble about their success. This is the type of person you could live next door to and never know they donated millions to charity until you read about it in their obituary.

As a date . . .
Because popcorn people are modest, they are never easy to get to know. They won't try to impress you and you won't be wowed on a date. However, once you get to know them, you will be surprised by their depth.

Popcorn-lovers are most compatible with other popcorn people, and they also mate well with pretzel-lovers.

What Does
Your Job
Reveal?

A couple of generations ago, it wouldn't have been possible to link professional choice and personality. A coal-miner's son tended to become a coal miner. Same for doctors, lawyers, accountants, and many other professions. Family-owned businesses were intended to be a legacy.

In many ways, this type of "career path" had its shortcomings because it restricted various groups in our society, most notably women and racial minorities. Nowadays, democracy and capitalism have opened up the opportunity to pursue happiness by allowing choice in career paths. We tend to be labeled and defined by our occupation. Our jobs or chosen paths in life, like our food preferences, are a reflection of our underlying essence—who we are. We eat who we are—and we work who we are. To paraphrase the philosopher Descartes, "I eat, therefore I am," or "I work, therefore I am."

> What you like to eat can
> even predict the career
> path you will follow.

Think about all the times you meet new people in social situations. It doesn't take long before you hear the question, "What do you do?" We always know what the question means. We don't say we ride bikes on weekends or love to

211

Snack Foods and Your Job

The following was gleaned in a study of 18,613 adult volunteers from thirty-three occupations who lived in the East and Midwest. It turned out that the most popular snack foods were potato chips and popcorn, and the least favorite were snack crackers and meat snacks. This is how it balanced out.

POTATO CHIPS	TORTILLA CHIPS	PRETZELS	CRACKERS
Lawyer	Farmer	Firefighter	Stockbroker
Tennis Pro	Travel Agent	Journalist	Professional Race-Car Driver
Police Officer	Chef	Flight Attendant	
	Clergy	Veterinarian	
CEO	News Anchor Person	Pediatrician	

CHEESE CURLS	MEAT SNACKS	NUTS	POPCORN
Real Estate Agent	Dentist	Architect	Artist
Psychiatrist	Bartender	Plumber	Teacher
Producer		Sanitation Worker	Truck Driver
		Cardiologist	Nurse
		Politician	Judge
			Neurosurgeon

read books and watch movies, even though these are things "we do."

Many factors influence career choices, including our economic and social status and our personal perception about the relative importance or prestige of a particular vocation. Obviously, individual ability comes into play. It's all well and good to be the daughter of a great tenor, but unless she is musically gifted as well, she won't make it in that field.

What's Their
Food Sign?

A strong correlation exists between personality characteristics and career choice, which is why guidance counselors and career-placement professionals use testing to help students and clients choose a profession. This is why timid people are not test pilots and why restless risk-takers are unhappy selling shoes. We have taken information to another dimension, and now can correlate career and food preference.

* CEOs and attorneys tend to be more driven or success-oriented than the average person, and we found predominately potato chip–lovers among them.

* Since perfectionists prefer tortilla chips, it is not surpris-

ing that professional chefs, travel agents, and news anchors are partial to them.

* Fun-loving, energetic, life-of-the-party pretzel-lovers confirm my experience in the social arena among firefighters, veterinarians, and pediatricians.

* Stockbrokers are contemplative and thoughtful snack cracker–lovers.

* The integrity of cheese curl–lovers makes them ideal real estate agents, psychiatrists, and producers.

* It makes sense that a bartender would prefer meat snacks, indicating a loyal and true friend.

* Nut-loving politicians interact well with the public in emergency situations.

* The self-confidence of those who prefer popcorn matches the career choice of neurosurgeons and judges.

Once we understand how accurately food preferences can predict personality traits, the guidance counselors in our high schools, not to mention dating services, will begin asking people about their "taste" in cuisine before advising them on career choices or matching them with a mate.

11

FRESHER THAN FRESH:
UP CLOSE AND PERSONAL

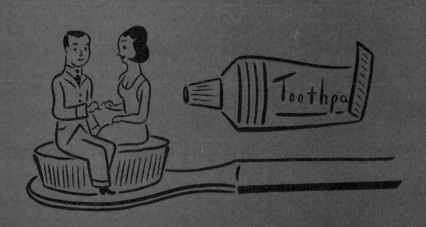

The scent of mint on your date's breath is just like a disguise. Find out what's behind the mask by checking what's in his pocket or in her purse.

• • • •

We make jokes about bad breath and good breath, but the scent of your breath takes on new meaning when it comes to courting romance. So it should come as no surprise to hear that breath fresheners are as common a commodity as hard candy. Many potential life-long love bonds failed due to one partner's less-than-pleasing breath. Your flavor in breath freshener speaks about you just as much as any of the foods discussed in this book.

By now this game is familiar to you. Before reading any further, answer the following. Which flavor of breath strips would you choose?

1) Peppermint
2) Fruit
3) Bubblegum
4) Spearmint
5) Wintergreen
6) Cinnamon

You Breathe
Who You Are

Early on in this book I discussed the role personal odor plays in romantic attraction. We can intuit a person's smell and unconsciously force a judgment—if we smell good, we must be good, and we believe the reverse to be true as well. Breath odor has a strong influence on our odor signature because our mouths are often close to people when we speak or breathe. The nose of the person sitting across the table from you is physically close enough to your mouth to pick up your odor signature.

> Breath mints can cover up your natural odor signature.

We decided to use breath strips because of their novelty and popularity. They are much like breath mints in that they come in a variety of flavors. Mint itself is viewed as a clean taste, and it may unconsciously make us feel cleaner and "good," at the same time making us more socially acceptable.

For this study, we recruited 430 men and women, both married and single, who followed the stringent personality testing we used in the previously described studies. Spearmint and cinnamon were the most popular flavors, with a combined total of 46 percent. The third and fourth most popular choices were peppermint and fruit flavor, at 20 percent each, followed by wintergreen (8 percent) and bubblegum (6 percent).

* **Intellectual types.** They enjoy working with computers, mathematics, or electronics—they may even be astronomers.

* **Creative.** They like having their own space so they can "create."

* **Watchers, not doers.** They like sports, but they'd rather watch than participate. Others might call them couch potatoes or armchair athletes.

Typical peppermints: Sandra Bullock's character in *The Net* or Michael Keaton as *Batman*.

Those who like peppermint are romantically compatible with those who prefer spearmint or cinnamon.

PEOPLE WHO PREFER
FRUIT ARE . . .

* **Steady and dependable.** They tend to be homebodies and enjoy safe, secure, close relationships.

* **Eager to please.** They tend to be followers rather than leaders. They're good team players, trying to please those around them.

* **Neutral.** They don't readily express their opinions for fear of hurting other people's feeling.

Typical fruits: Bill Murray's character in *What about Bob?*, Tom Hanks's character in *Forrest Gump,* and Renée Zellweger's character in *Bridget Jones's Diary.*

Those who prefer fruit flavor are most romantically compatible with those who prefer peppermint or wintergreen.

PEOPLE WHO PREFER BUBBLEGUM ARE . . .

* **Action-oriented.** They enjoy both physical and mental challenges, and are the "doers" of the world.

* **Self-confident.** They are intuitive, goal-oriented, and always in control (though, at times, they can be impulsive).

Typical bubblegums: Anthony Hopkins's character in *Silence of the Lambs* and Richard Gere's character in *Chicago.*

Bubblegum-lovers are best partnered with those who prefer peppermint or wintergreen.

WHAT'S YOUR FOOD SIGN?

* **Immaculate dressers.** They are also fond of wearing expensive jewelry, or at least jewelry that looks expensive.

* **Authoritative and powerful.** They tend to take charge in any situation, which makes them good leaders. They are, however, sensitive to criticism.

Typical spearmints: The character of James Bond.

Those who prefer spearmint are most romantically compatible with individuals who prefer peppermint.

* **Self-critical.** They have high expectations of themselves, and therefore are tough self critics.

* **Overly sensitive.** They are easily offended by even relatively trivial remarks, and often misinterpret what others say.

* **Easily embarrassed.** But among close friends, they are animated and fun.

Typical wintergreens: Jim Carrey's character in *The Truman Show* or *The Mask,* and Charlie Brown in *Peanuts.*

Wintergreen-lovers are most romantically compatible with other wintergreens but also get along well with those who prefer cinnamon and fruit flavor.

PEOPLE WHO PREFER CINNAMON ARE . . .

* **Novelty cravers.** They enjoy new and exciting adventures.

* **Fashion lovers.** And they choose all the right accessories!

* **Flirtatious.** They are provocative and love having a good time.

Typical cinnamons: Goldie Hawn's character in *Private Benjamin* and Chevy Chase's character in *Fletch.*

Those who prefer cinnamon are best suited to the more grounded peppermint-lover.

So, You're Out on a Date . . .

Pinpointing your date's taste in breath freshener can be a little tough, because it isn't something two people generally share when they go out, especially in a new relationship.

You can try asking, "Got a mint?" and you might get your answer easily. Just don't say, "Want a mint?" or you could be history real fast. You should carry your favorite flavor with you, though, in case an appropriate opportunity comes up to fit it casually into your conversation.

There are some behaviors that can tip you in the right direction:

. . . .

A peppermint personality could:

* Divide her/his attention by checking the score of the game on the TV set at the bar.

* Talk about how much she/he likes to hang out at home.

* Have a serious job like an engineer or a scientist.

. . . .

A fruit personality could:

* Dress kind of dull.

* Ask a lot about you and reveal little about himself.

* Talk about hearth and home as being all-important.

. . . .

A bubblegum personality could:

* Rush you into the restaurant like this date is just another thing on her/his busy to-do list.

* Spot a pool table in the bar and ask you for a challenge.

. . . .

A spearmint personality could:

* Wear a lot of expensive jewelry.

* Speak with an authoritative air about everything under the sun.

. . . .

A wintergreen personality could:

* Take what you say the wrong way and get offended easily.

* Turn out to be a good friend.

· ·

A cinnamon personality could:

* Be sporting a great tan she/he got on an adventure trip to some exotic place.

* Be impeccably dressed, down to the perfect necktie or accessories.

· ·

The Toothpaste
Challenge

Chose your favorite toothpaste flavor.

1. Cinnamon-mint
2. Citrus (orange-peppermint)
3. Herbal mint
   (spearmint-anise-thyme)

Like our food choices, our toothpaste choice represents far more than the couple of seconds we spend making our pick at the drugstore or supermarket. Subconscious factors also come into play. Our choice of toothpaste is influenced by the image projected through its marketing and advertisements. So, just as "we eat what we are," you can likewise say, we "brush what we are." We choose toothpaste so that we may become the essence of what it is, based on perceptions we unconsciously hold about its qualities.

> We choose toothpaste so that we may become the essence of what it is.

Excluding the rationale based on dental hygiene, we likely choose toothpaste based on flavor preference. The sense of smell is important, too, although we may not be conscious of it. We recruited 535 adults for our study, and we compared flavor preferences between spouses. Most people preferred herbal mint (63 percent), followed by cinnamon-mint (34 percent) and citrus (3 percent).

WHAT'S YOUR FOOD SIGN?

We formulated the results based on this forced-choice, ten-question test. Take the test yourself and see where you fall. Choose only one answer per question.

	A	**B**	**C**
1. I daydream.	Frequently	Sometimes	Never
2. I am confident in myself.	Very	Somewhat	Not very
3. I am impatient.	Very	Somewhat	Not very
4. I am sensitive to criticism.	Very	Somewhat	Not very
5. I am competitive.	Very	Somewhat	Not very
6. I am punctual.	Almost always	Usually	Rarely
7. I abide by the rules.	Sometimes	Usually	Always
8. In my dwelling, one could "eat off the floor."	Only If starving and the food is gourmet	Only if really hungry	Without fear of getting ill
9. I am a pack rat.	Never	Sometimes	Often
10. I am extravagant.	Frequently	Occasionally	Almost never

Total Number:

FRESHER THAN FRESH

* **If your answer was "A" five** or more times, the tooth-paste flavor that fits your personality is herbal mint.

* **If your answer was "B" five** or more times, the tooth-paste flavor that most suits your personality is citrus.

* **If your answer was "C" five** or more times, the tooth-paste flavor that most suits your personality is cinna-mon-mint.

* **If you don't have five** in any single column or you have five in two different columns, your flavor prefer-ences cannot be reliably predicted.

WHO'S COMPATIBLE
WITH WHOM

* **Those who prefer cinnamon-mint** are most compat-ible with others who prefer cinnamon-mint and herbal mint.

* **Those who prefer citrus** are most compatible with others who prefer citrus.

* **Those who prefer herbal mint** are universal roman-tics—they are compatible with anyone no matter what their toothpaste flavor preference.

You Take My Breath Away

We like to smell "fresh and clean," and using toothpaste, breath mints, and breath strips are popular ways to achieve this (second probably only to bathing). Even if you wake up late and don't have time for a shower, you still brush your teeth. Even if you don't wear perfume, you brush your teeth. If you eat onions or garlic for lunch, you pop a mint or a breath strip before your after-lunch encounter with friends or coworkers.

These minty refreshers, however, can interfere with your ability to truly get to know someone because they mask a person's true underlying essence or unique odor signature. You're left to sniff out your fresh-breathed date's flavor choice to help you determine some of his/her core personality traits. Considering how common freshening one's breath is, it is an easy and quick food sign.

12

YOU *CAN* UNDERSTAND YOUR PARTNER

It goes without saying that the better you understand the person you are dating, the faster you will get to know each other and decide if you are meant for each other.

• • • • •

This does not mean that two people are not ideal for each other because he drinks black coffee and she likes latte. What your date orders for lunch or dinner is never "wrong."

Everything that food reveals about the special someone you are with provides another clue as to his or her inner essence. Rarely will a person fit snugly into one personality type. We can adjust to a variety of personality types if we accept people for who they are rather than trying to change them into what we want them to be. Morning people can live happily with night owls once they get over the notion that couples are supposed to live on the same schedule. Much of the difficulty we face in relationships comes from hanging on to preconceived notions of what we're conditioned to think is "right" and "wrong." This is why couples end up arguing rather than communicating.

> Anyone can be your fit as long as you accept who they are instead of trying to change them into who you want them to be.

As a relationship progresses, you will discover certain personality characteristics that you didn't see earlier. Some of them may not please you. This is why looking for early clues about personality are important: they will help you avoid surprises, hopefully before it's too late.

Throughout this book, we've looked at food preferences, and then linked them to personality. Here this process is reversed. This list of personality traits matches a variety of foods we found people with these traits prefer. It's logical to flip the information this way because when we think of the type of person we want to marry, we think it terms of the qualities that are important to us. However, we don't necessarily think carefully about this. We all say we want someone who is "kind," "fun-loving," and has "a good sense of humor." But you never hear someone say: "I'd like to meet an aggressive, impatient person who is a natural leader and has a flair for the dramatic."

This is a list of some of the qualities that are important to most people, even if they don't openly express it, matched with some of the foods discussed in this book.

Loyal
In a vodka bar these men and women would choose the orange flavor, and on a hot day might offer you a lemonade. They tend to like lattes, although you might see them drinking a tea-based frap. They probably prefer meat snacks over pretzels or chips, and like their cheese in cubes. They may pull out fruit-flavored breath strips and you could find cinnamon-flavored toothpaste in their bathrooms.

Perfectionist and Conservative
Both of these types may reach for the tortilla chips or cheese curls to go with their iced tea with lemon, and they tend to like foods seasoned with intense spices such as curry powder, cayenne pepper, crushed red pepper, chili powder, and mixed peppers. They prefer their cheese in cubes.

Energetic
These people put plain yellow mustard on their burgers, but they prefer their cheese in either stars or moon shapes or

shreds. You'll make them happy if you put out a bowl of pretzels, and they're happy if you have either vanilla or double chocolate chunk ice cream in the freezer. They'll likely order a coffee frap or a latte, but in the evening they could choose either decaf iced tea or peach vodka. If you meet for breakfast, they'll order pancakes.

Ambitious

These men and women like their coffee black but will enjoy a coffee frap as a change of pace. They eat potato chips and would choose the cranberry in a vodka bar. They like fruit—oranges, bananas, and grapes—and when they order ice cream, they can't make up their minds between chocolate chip and mint chocolate chip.

Shy

Shy men and women might keep snack crackers and strawberry ice cream handy, along with packages of cheese in sunburst shapes. You may also find them snacking on cherries or pumpkin pie.

Forward-Thinking

Those who plan ahead snack on cheese curls and cheese cubes, and they tend toward mint chocolate chip ice cream. You might find citrus breeze toothpaste in their bathroom.

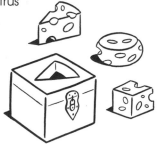

Loner

Those who enjoy being alone like snack crackers topped with cheese shaped like sunbursts and a glass of pink lemonade to go with it. You may find them seasoning dinner with garlic, pepper, clove, sage, or saffron.

Seductive and Dramatic

These personality types choose green tea with peach, and are partial to banana nut bread. They'll choose Good & Plenty candy, coffee ice cream, cheese shaped like stars and moons. They like their food spicy, and you can find onion salt, celery salt, celery seed, garlic salt, and pickling spices in their pantry. You may also find them ordering chai tea.

Adventurous

Those with a spirit for adventure love vanilla ice cream and cream-based fraps, and they freshen their breath with either bubblegum or cinnamon strips. When it comes to spices, they're similar to their dramatic, seductive cousins and prefer onion and celery salt, celery seed, garlic salt, and pickling spices.

Trendy

Those on the trendy side will freshen their breath with cinnamon or spearmint strips and eat cheese in the shapes of stars and moons or in shreds. They snack on pretzels, and if they have ice cream in the freezer, it's likely double chocolate chunk.

Contemplative and Thoughtful

These individuals like vegetables and favor corn, eggplant, and tomatoes. They also eat snack crackers and their favorite ice cream is strawberry. They like tea or fruit-based fraps, and their favorite sweets may be pumpkin pie, black licorice, and doughnuts.

Extroverted

Extroverts like their cheese in the traditional shredded variety and you might see them drinking peach-flavored green tea while munching pretzels.

Easy-Going

The easy-going among us like to snack on nuts, perhaps with a glass of lemonade or a cocktail made with orange vodka. They like banana cream pie and creamed corn, applesauce, and pineapple chunks. These men and women like to spice their foods with parsley, chives, paprika, bay leaves, and sweet basil.

Leader

Those who lead tend to choose raspberry as their favorite vodka and lemonade, and like their sandwiches with a slice of cheese. They like rocky road ice cream, and are partial to fruit such as oranges, bananas, and grapes. They freshen their breath with spearmint strips. They favor spices like carroway seed, fennel, mint, anise seed, and nutmeg.

Social

Those who consider themselves social beings like meat snacks, vanilla vodka, chocolate ice cream, decaf iced tea, cranberries, and pink grapefruit.

Competitive

Competitive individuals like butter pecan ice cream and cheese in slices. They're likely to use herbal mint toothpaste.

Confident

You'll find men and women with confidence sipping on raspberry vodka, and they may snack on popcorn.

Men and women often have trouble interacting because they may say things they don't mean. They "go along to get along"—at least at first. A person who seems unusually shy and retiring can turn out to be a loving and reliable partner. The super-charming man or woman who seems irresistible may be a good actor with shallow character. Even in the absence of such extremes, problems start to crop up when the façade starts to fade and people begin to reveal their true needs and desires and, of course, they expect their partners to accept the "real" self. This is where a kind of "divorce" takes place in many relationships, and it's certainly when partners may think— or say—"You aren't who I thought you were."

Food preferences provide insights into the real self that a person consciously or unconsciously does not show or does not want to show when you first meet. The above list of personality traits can give you a quick take to find out if what you're seeing is really

237

what you're getting. It does not mean that someone is trying to trick you, especially on a conscious level. It isn't a question of tricking them to reveal something negative about themselves, either. Rather, it is a question of understanding another's wants and desires. Those falling in love want to please, and in doing so can misinterpret or misrepresent. Then, they don't understand why tensions eventually develop.

> Food preferences provide insight into the real self that a person consciously or unconsciously is not showing.

For example, someone who loves cheese curls has high integrity, but also likes their home spotlessly clean, a trait you find annoying. If you know that about another person, you can weigh your options. You could decide to learn to live with that trait, perhaps agreeing to do your fair share, or maybe you can compromise—you cook and he or she cleans. You just shouldn't expect the person to change. If it's a trait that you find too difficult to live with, then you are better off moving on. But, if the relationship matters to you, you can negotiate a solution.

It is essential to approach dating and romance with good humor and acceptance. Too often men and women find that as a couple they lack a certain "spark" or they realize that their differences aren't complementary. Then they break up, leaving one or both partners with bad feelings. They could, however, become friends or friendly acquaintances or even allies in their search for someone else. At the very least, they should extend good will to each other.

It is critical to never judge any individual's personality trait or traits as "wrong." Everyone has gifts and qualities that make him or her unique. You should approach dating with the attitude that the person you're meeting for coffee or lunch or sharing your popcorn with at the movies deserves your respect. It isn't easy to put everything on the line and be vulnerable, which is why it is important to show generosity of spirit to each other.

This book is meant to be an informative and light-hearted look at a serious subject. Perhaps no subject is more serious than finding a partner with whom you can share the often challenging journey through life. On the other hand, romance is supposed to be fun and one of the most satisfying experiences one will every have. That said, I invite you to enjoy this book. And good luck on your quest for lasting love.

Acknowledgments

With gratitude to all whose assistance has been invaluable in the production of this book: Michele Oliver and Denise Fahey, for their daily Herculean efforts; Virginia McCullough for her literary and inspirational insights; Debora Yost at Stewart, Tabori & Chang for her valued editorial suggestions; and my literary agent, Noah Lukeman, for finding a home for this book.

Special thanks to Debra, Marissa, Jack, Camryn, and Noah, who were willing to sacrifice our time together so that I could complete this book.

My thanks to all.

—A. R. H.

• •

For information about disorders of smell or taste, including reduced or increased ability to smell or taste, odd or distorted smells or tastes, or burning mouth syndrome, contact the Smell & Taste Treatment and Research Foundation at 845 N. Michigan Ave., 900W, Chicago, IL 60611, or at www.smellandtaste.org.

To obtain Timeless View, a grapefruit-based perfume that reduces the perceived age of women, log on to www.scienceofsmell.com or www.smellandtaste.org.

For more information on the KFC condiment flavor preferences as they relate to personality, log on to www.KFC.com.

For information on using smells for weight loss, sexual arousal, learning, or the perception of weight, log on to www.smellandtaste.org or www.scienceofsmell.com.

For more details about the study of personality and ice cream preferences, log on to www.icecream.com.

Previous books by Alan R. Hirsch (available at www.smellandtaste.org):

> *Scentsational Weight Loss*
> *Scentsational Sex*
> *What Flavor Is Your Personality?*
> *Life's a Smelling Success*
> *What Your Doctor May Not Tell You about Sinusitis*